The Bible on Abortion

The shedding of innocent blood

Bruce Benson

The Bible on Abortion

The shedding of innocent blood

Published by Heart Wish Books
Cambridge, Massachusetts

heartwishbooks@gmail.com

All Bible quotations are the author's paraphrase unless marked

Bible quotations marked (KJV) are from
the King James Version in the public domain

Library of Congress Control Number: 2021904208

ISBN: 9780999803981

Religion – Christian theology – Ethics
Religion – Christian life – Women's issues

Other books by Bruce Benson

AHA moments from the Bible

Jehovah's Witnesses Hate Jehovah

Gay-affirming theology: An explicit exposé

The Catholic Church: femme fatale

Bible Talk: 50 literal drawings explained

Try my Bible Quiz

Speaking in tongues: Shamana bo-ho roe-toe

Joseph Reflects Jesus: Lifegivers

Otros libros del autor en español

La Biblia sobre el Aborto: El derramamiento de sangre inocente

Momentos AJÁ de la Biblia

Los Testigos de Jehová odian a Jehová

Teología de la validación gay: Una exposición explícita

La Iglesia Católica: mujer fatal

Charla sobre la Biblia: 50 dibujos literales explicados

¡Prueba mi cuestionario bíblico!

Hablar en lenguas: Shamana bo-jo ro-to

José refleja a Jesús: Dadores de vida

Contents

Chapter One

Simple facts

A few words first

Here's the plan –
We'll just talk for a while. I did the work for you. Relax and read. Then we come to Chapter Four. It has a lot of Bible. Does that turn you off? Well, you are reading a book called The Bible on Abortion. And in Chapter Four I'll need you to let God save your soul.

In Chapter Seven I'll show you how to do the work. I need you to start doing serious Bible study. Then there will be one less person in the world who says things they don't understand because they don't study the Bible.

On my answers to the abortion questions –
You might think the answers can't be so simple. But they are. And they fit in this small book. Yes, the answers are simple. But it takes a lot of hard work to extract the answers from the Bible and present them to people in a way they can understand them. Thank God if He gives you that work. It's the greatest journey. You'll discover the most precious treasures. They will transform you. And you'll learn that true love is sharing those treasures with others.

Why do I do my own paraphrases?
A paraphrase is when you say, "In other words…" I put Bible verses in other words – in words most people understand. I untangle the knots and smooth out the verses – to make them easier to read – to make the meaning easier to see – and to make it easier for you to get enjoyment and satisfaction from the Bible. That's the job of qualified Christians. We all need people who do that. It helps us with our own work.

Am I qualified to do paraphrases? Yes. God gave me His Holy Spirit, a ministry, and spiritual gifts. And I've been a serious student of the Bible for many years.

My hope is that God will speak to you and change your heart. All of us need God to cleanse our sinful hearts.

Bruce Benson

What's the right question?

Where's the verse in the Bible that says do not abort?

There is no verse. There is a verse that says do not murder a person. The only way abortion could be lawful then is if a fetus is a thing, like used toilet paper. If a fetus is a person then there's no need for a verse that says do not abort.

Is a fetus a person? That's the right question.

Where's the verse in the Bible that says a fetus is a person?

There is no verse. There's no need for it. When God talks about a fetus He uses the same words and expresses the same feelings as when He talks about people who've been born. God feels the same way about you aborting a fetus as He would if you hacked your five-year-old daughter to death.

I've given you the conclusion up front.

In chapter nine you'll see how God taught us that a fetus is a person (pages 95 to 102).

A child enters the womb at conception and goes from one-celled zygote, to embryo, and then fetus. I'll be using the word fetus for a child in the womb from conception to birth.

Do not murder a person.
God, Exodus 20:13

Can you determine when life begins?

What's that? You can't determine when life begins? Oh, but God said you can. You know it when you see it. God gave you two eyes, a brain, and a conscience. That's all you need. God knows you're lying.

And you've had the advantage of access to the knowledge God gave us in the Bible – plus a brilliant mind, the best education money can buy, authority, influence, and exceptional speaking skills. Imagine what you could have done to rescue the children. You failed. God hates it when you pretend not to know that innocent people are being led to their death.

You can't determine when life begins? So, you're admitting that they might be alive. Then you should be crying out for an immediate halt to all abortions until you can determine. What if they are alive? What if they feel it? You don't know when life begins but you grin and bless abortion. That's cold.

You're making light of something God takes very seriously. The God you say you believe in values human life. You show a reckless disregard for human life – deliberate negligence.

On Judgment Day you'll have no trouble determining how angry God is with you.

> Innocent people are being executed.
> You see them trembling as they're hauled off to be slaughtered.
> But you don't grab hold of them and pull them away.
> You don't yell – Stop!
> You look the other way.
> You don't save their life.
> Then you say, "I didn't know."
> The One who saves your life knows.
> God searches through your thoughts and feelings.
> And God pays back everyone for what they do.
> Proverbs 24:11-12

Chapter Two

What is abortion?

Names used in this book

The expression pro-choice was designed to hide the truth.

I'll be dealing with reality. Abortion is the bloody murder of a child. Instead of pro-choice, I'll call them what God calls them. I'll call them the Bloodyhands.

> I will not listen to you when you pray
> because your hands are full of blood.
> God, Isaiah 1:15

My name for those who oppose abortion is the Speakfors.

> Speak up for those who are unable to speak.
> Proverbs 31:8

An act of cruelty

Abortion is legal because people in authority said a child in the womb
is not a person. That's why politicians can say a child in the womb has
no legal rights and can be killed right up to the day of delivery – that
they can be murdered on their birthday.

Here's the truth. If you're human then you're a person. And you have
the God-given right to live. A child in the womb is a person. That's
proved by the Bible and by science. And it's proved from observation
and experience. There's no such thing as a child who is not a person.

You're either 100% a person or you're 0% a person. There's no such
thing as a 75% person. So, if you say a fetus is not a person then you're
saying a fetus is a thing.

Then why do you Bloodyhands hide aborted fetuses? If you really
believed a fetus is not a person then you'd use them to pay for
abortions. You'd stuff them and sell them as dolls. You'd grind them
up for pig food or textile industry.

If you really believed a fetus is a thing then you'd fund your operation
by selling aborted fetuses to the billion dollar porn industry. Fetus
porn. Isn't that child porn? Not according to very smart people in
positions of authority. They told us a fetus is no different than a dildo.

What's that, Bloodyhands? Porn is evil? Oh, so you know porn is evil
but you think it's okay to murder a baby? That's your idea of right and
wrong?

You won't use fetuses for footballs because you know what they are.
That's why you get rid of their bodies. So people won't know that
you're killing children.

Wicked people hide in secret places to murder the innocent.
Psalm 10:8

Are you shocked and disgusted? Good.

Don't get me wrong. Porn is evil. I'm making a point. The Bloodyhands tell you abortion is a good thing, a thing blessed by God. I want you to know how evil it is – like child porn is evil. A fetus is not a thing. They are a person.

You need to know this. They're little people. Real people are being killed in the most shocking and cruel ways. Abortion is the killing of children. If you saw an abortion performed you would immediately become a Speakfor.

You Bloodyhands can hide but you're not fooling God.

When Cain murdered his brother Abel, God said this to Cain –

> What have you done? I can hear the voice of your
> brother's blood crying out to Me from the ground.
> God, Genesis 4:10

You pour the blood of aborted babies down the drain. But God hears their blood crying out to Him from the sewer.

Abel was a good man. He loved God.

> To God, the death of those who love Him is very costly.
> Psalm 116:15

And here you are, you Bloodyhands, taking it into your hands to kill people who love God. God knows them and loves them. You have no right to kill them. How would you feel if someone murdered a person you love? Now imagine how God feels about those He loves being aborted. He's angry. God avenges their deaths.

> Vengeance is Mine. I will retaliate, says the Lord.
> Romans 12:19

One day at my street ministry two young women were reading my pamphlet about abortion. A man saw them reading it. He told them he worked in an abortion clinic. He assured them that what's removed from a woman during an abortion is just something like a heavy (menstrual) period. They believed him.

Do you want to know how much of a lie that is? Do you want to know how cruel abortion is? There's something you could do if you have any doubts. You could go online. There are sites that show you photos. You can see what a child looks like after they've been aborted. You see dead children. But not just dead. These children have clearly been tortured to death. It will haunt you.

One method of abortion is called Suction Abortion. It's done in the first few months of pregnancy. They vacuum the baby out. You can see the results. Arms, legs, and hands, all in a pile like at a meat market.

The Bloodyhands don't want the woman to think there's a child in her womb. So, they won't use the word child. And they won't use the word pregnancy. Instead, they refer to the time of her pregnancy as the time since her last menstrual period. The child is ignored. They don't show the woman what the child in her womb looks like. And they don't show her photos of what the child will look like after the abortion.

They don't say they're going to use a sharp object to rip the child from her womb, destroy the child's body and kill the child. Instead they tell the woman they'll be using gentle suction to empty her uterus.

> The Lord hates bloody and deceitful people.
> Psalm 5:6

When the child has been in the womb for more than a few months they use a method called Dilation and Evacuation. They insert sharp tools into the womb to grab and twist the baby's body parts. The baby is torn apart limb from limb – then taken from the womb piece by piece. It might also be necessary to crush the child's skull in order to remove it. That's a child. Will you please look at the photos.

Another horror is called Saline Amniocentesis or saline-injection abortion. Basically, they kill the child with salt.

A child in the womb lives inside a bag of water. The Bloodyhands stick a needle in the bag to remove some of the life-giving water that surrounds the child. Then they replace it with salt water. The baby writhes in pain until they die.

There are photos. You see a dead child. You see how their little body was burned from the salt. Imagine if they did that to you. You'd scream and thrash until you died. It's no different for the child in the womb.

There are other methods. But the most evil might be the Partial-Birth Abortion. This happens in the last months. They insert pliers into the womb and use them to pull the baby out. But they leave the baby's head inside the mother.

They cut a hole in the baby's head and insert a tube. They suck out the baby's brains. The baby's skull collapses. Then they remove the baby's head from the womb. They call it a legal abortion because they left the child's head in the womb when they killed the child.

You know about these things. And yet you have the nerve to say you can't determine when life begins.

How cruel is abortion? What if you had a golden retriever dog. You've had her since she was born. You always treated her well. She trusts you completely, adores you, would die for you. But one day you take a knife and stab her in the eye. Imagine how she would feel. The confusion, the pain. Oh, she'd forgive you and blame the knife.

If we wouldn't do that to the dogs we consider to be members of the family then how can we do it to a child?

Ancient Rome killed people by nailing them to a cross. Before the condemned person was crucified they were given a drink laced with a narcotic. It dulled the pain.   Matthew 27:34

Children who are aborted are worse off than those who were tortured to death by cruel Rome. No compassionate person is let into the abortion factory to give them something to dull the pain of the abortion. Their executioners don't give them anything.

Have you ever tried to pull your own tooth with a pair of pliers? You can't because it hurts too much. So you stop. Then you go to a dentist who gives you an injection so you won't feel the pain of the extraction. You had the freedom, the choice to go to the dentist. The child in the womb is just like us. They feel the same pain we feel. But they have no choice. The pain and death of abortion is forced on them.

Children who are aborted are treated like cattle in a slaughterhouse. They're subjected to the most extreme pain with no anesthetic. Their brains are wrecked. Their heartbeats are stopped. They bleed to death. They have little faces, fingers and toes that are all torn apart. Imagine what the child feels during an abortion. Imagine the shock, the fear. They're being murdered. In the place they felt safe and nurtured.

We know they have feelings. They respond to stimulus. It means they feel pain.

Oh, you say, it's a known fact that children in the womb don't feel pain until after two or three months in the womb. Oh, so you're against aborting after two or three months? But how could you risk hurting a child? How sick is it to think it's okay to kill a child because you think they can't feel it?

What if someone said dogs don't feel pain and they hurt your dog? You'd want to kill them. Children being aborted feel it just like you'd feel it if you were skinned alive. You think they can't feel it? Then look please, online, at ultrasounds of children in the womb. Then tell me it's okay to kill him.

When a mother gives birth she's offered something for the pain. No such consideration is given to the child when a mother decides to abort. Of course they feel pain. They have a brain, a heart, and blood flowing through their little body.

During World War Two surgery was performed on people with no anesthesic, no pain killer. They would rape and impregnate a woman. Then, after the baby in her womb was several months along, they would strap her down and operate on her with no pain killer. She was wide awake during the surgery. This was done for research.

Yes, it was unimaginably cruel. But it happened. And that's what's being done to children during an abortion. A human being is tortured to death in an unimaginably cruel way. If you're pro-choice, then you're no better than the ones who operated on those women.

How does it make you feel when you hear that someone was decapitated in an accident? Now think about the children, thousands every week, deliberately mutilated. You think factory farming is cruel? If you saw what goes on in an abortion factory you'd want to kill yourself.

There are politicians who celebrate abortion. Then they say they look out for the little guy. But they're the biggest bullies on the block. Children in the womb are the littlest little guy. Children in the womb are being bullied to death.

Every human being is 100% a person from the moment of conception to the moment of their death – regardless of their size, their physical shape, their I.Q., their abilities, or lack of abilities. No one has a right to oppress them, bully them, or murder them. Abortion's not a fair fight. You're picking on someone smaller than you.

God doesn't make you pass a test to be a person. You're still a person if you can't hit a baseball or solve a math problem. And God sees the person in the womb the same as He sees us. My point is this – people will try to come up with their own idea of when we become a person. They do that because they want to say that yes, a fetus is alive, a fetus is human, but they're not a person, so it's okay to abort them.

If that were the case then next they could say it's okay to kill people in a coma or people who are elderly or disabled or dying.

Justice is supposed to be blind. It means justice looks at the crime, not at the person. Justice isn't supposed to let someone get away with a crime because they're rich or famous. And it's not supposed to deny justice to someone because of their physical appearance. But that's what abortion does.

Every nation, every society forbids murder and punishes those who commit murder. Why is the murder of children in the womb permitted? It's because they're too little, too unimportant. Abortion is as bad as racial hatred. The Bloodyhands see children in the womb as different. The Bloodyhands think they're better than the children in the womb. They think that makes it okay to kill them. Children in the womb are the most oppressed minority. It's killing them.

Children in the womb are discriminated against because of where they live. If you kill a baby after it comes out of the womb you'll be charged with murder. But seconds earlier it was legal to kill that very same baby. In seconds their value changed.

So, I have a question. Are you able to determine if life has begun in a newborn baby? Yes? But a few seconds earlier, when that very same baby was in the womb, you said you were unable to determine. Here's my question – do you want to change your answer?

Hundreds of millions of lives have been stolen by abortion. What would their voices have sounded like? What would their smile look like? They might have made great discoveries, great contributions to science or the military. They might have been your friend or spouse.

Every sports record should have an asterisk. This record was achieved by an unfair advantage – millions of potential competitors were murdered.* This is worse than the murderous tyrants of the twentieth century. Wars are fought over this kind of thing. This is a most serious and urgent matter.

What fools we are to ignore it. How selfish of us. We close our eyes. The Bloodyhands are so vicious and vengeful. They've made people afraid to speak up.

Psychologists must have a name for it. When people hear someone being murdered but are so afraid to get involved they won't even call the police.

There should be a strike. Athletes and actors should refuse to perform. Stadiums and theaters should close. People should walk out of work and school. There should be tens of millions marching through the streets. Then things would change.

Turn on your TV to any morning news show. You'll hear people engaged in the most useless chatter, ignoring the children who will be killed that day by abortion.

Imagine how children in the womb would feel if they knew that we know they're being tortured to death but we ignore them. How would they feel if they knew that while they're being burned and ripped apart, we're cheering on a sports team or laughing along with our favorite TV comedy. Now imagine how God feels about us.

Why does it continue? Corrupt politicians. Fake preachers. Apathy. Fear of persecution. It's out of sight and out of mind. People are brainwashed by the lying arguments. This is one of the worst things that's ever happened. The children need someone to save them. What's needed is mourning and repentance.

The news media is complicit in the murder of children. They keep it hidden by remaining silent about it. What if every night on the news they showed film of children in the womb and then showed photos of children after they're aborted?

> We interrupt this program to bring you a bulletin.
> We've just received word that hundreds of children
> were brutally murdered today.

What if they reported how many children were killed each day and graphically described how those children were killed? If the media told it like it is, then people would take to the streets in protest, as many as when a sports team wins a championship.

The news media love to tell us about a dog that was abused. People go crazy – they cry and wail. They're filled with anger, and they want severe, swift punishment. They love to end the news with a heartwarming story, like when the dog was swimming out to sea and was rescued. But children being tortured to death goes ignored.

The news media are bad Samaritans. They look the other way.

There have been women who were pregnant and planned to get an abortion but for one reason or another they didn't. Those children who weren't aborted have grown up to be adults and live among us. What would have happened if women who <u>did</u> get an abortion had <u>also</u> not gotten an abortion for one reason or another? Then those children also would have grown up to be adults and live among us.

How can you say abortion is okay because you can't determine when life begins? Even if you think a fetus is not a person, you know it will become a person. How can you kill something you know will become a person? No. It doesn't matter if you can't determine when life begins. You're killing something you know will become a person. Therefore, you're willfully killing a person.

You know people are being murdered but you plead ignorance.

Abortion is not done in the heat of passion. The abortionist lies in wait to kill the child. Deadly weapons are used. The abortion is done by people who are called sane. There's no insanity defense. Abortion is a planned and premeditated killing of a human being. I'd call that first degree murder.

What if a child survives the abortion? You'd think that child would be granted a pardon by the governor. You'd think there would be a celebration in the abortion factory.

You would think they'd immediately wrap the child in a blanket and nurture them. No, none of that happens. The child is left to die alone on a cold metal table. No one can touch the child. The Bloodyhands carry out the death sentence one way or another.

People who are aborted have not committed a death penalty offense. God said the governnment can't execute someone without a trial. Before the state can execute a person they must first prove the person's guilt beyond a reasonable doubt. Aborted children are denied due process.

On the testimony of two witnesses.
Deuteronomy 17:6

The child is not given their day in court, not read their rights, not given one phone call, not told what crime they've committed. No trial, no witnesses, no jury of their peers, no appeal, no mercy. The child can't request an attorney, can't cry out for justice. Abortion is cruel and unusual punishment.

They can't wait to shed innocent blood.
Isaiah 59:7

A child in the womb has no choice, no vote, no rights, no armed defenders to burst in and rescue them. They're denied their right to free speech and expression of religion. They're denied their God-given right to life, their right to self-defense, their right to bear arms.

The aborted child is given nothing before they're executed – no last meal, no cigarette, no blindfold. God hates injustice. He will avenge that child's unlawful execution.

Evil workers sentence the innocent to death.
Psalm 94:21

Nehemiah 9:19 tells us of the great compassion that God feels for those He loves. In the King James Version the word for God's compassion is – mercies. It's #7356 in the Strong's Concordance. The word for God's compassion also means womb. God intended the womb to be the place where a child is shown tender love.

Abortion is when a mother kills her own child.

A woman I know told me that years ago she thought she was going to die when she was giving birth to her child. But her only thought was for her child's safe birth.

Unless you were raped you chose to do something that resulted in that child being in your womb. You have a moral obligation now to protect them and let them be born. That's what Jesus said you must do. Even if you got pregnant from rape, Jesus loves that child.

Children's rights come first. That's how it works. The strong protect the weak. Parents protect children. If parents hears gunshots they don't use their child as a shield to protect themselves. They throw themselves over the child's body. They don't think twice. They're willing to die so their child can live.

Men and women in the military sacrifice themselves in war for God, for their loved ones, for their family, and for their country so people can live in freedom. Police, firefighters, and other first responders sacrifice themselves to protect all of us, including people they don't even know, for people who don't care about them, even for people who hate them. Jesus sacrificed His life for all of us.

In John 15:13 Jesus said the greatest love is when someone sacrifices their life so those they love can live.

The baby in your womb is not asking you to die for them. They're just asking you to not kill them.

The child in your womb needs you to love them.

Abortion is no way to treat a person.

Chapter Three

Their lying arguments

How do they lie to you?

The Bloodyhands trick you by changing the meaning of words. They can't say they're in favor of torturing a child to death, so they call it women's health care. It's what magicians do. Look over here so you don't see the dead child.

The devil's greatest magic trick is getting people to accept an evil thing by making them think it's a good thing.

Genesis 3:1-13; Isaiah 5:20; 2 Corinthians 11:13-15

Deceivers don't tell obvious lies. They blend lies with truth to create lies that sound right.

A politician tells you the law must allow a woman to abort her baby up to the day of delivery. Why? Because there are countries where women are forced to <u>not</u> give birth and countries where women are forced <u>to</u> give birth. They gave you a truth. There are places in the world where women are treated like that. Where's the lie? The untrained eye won't see it.

In my book, Jehovah's Witnesses hate Jehovah, I introduced you to our Guide – the truth found in the Bible that Jesus is God. This time our Guide will be the truth found in the Bible that a fetus is a person.

Our Guide reveals the hidden lie that was slipped in with the truth. The lie is in what the politician didn't tell you – abortion kills a person.

Our Guide will expose the Bloodyhand's arguments for what they are. Lying arguments, every one of them.

Choice

The expression pro-choice is a wolf in sheep's clothing. Killing a baby sounds so awful.

What pro-choice people don't tell you is that only one side gets to choose. It's not a choice when one person has all the power and the other person has none. The mother is given the choice to kill the child. But the child is not given the choice to kill the mother. That's not choice. That's just murder.

You want choice? Then be fair. Let the child be born and give them the right to choose to kill you. When they're eighteen you can challenge them to a duel. But have your hands tied behind your back first so you know how a child in the womb feels.

Choice doesn't change law. The Bible says choice doesn't make rape okay. The government's job is to protect a woman's choice to not be raped. The Bible says choice doesn't make murder okay. The government's job is to protect a child's choice to not be aborted.

Genesis 9:6; Exodus 20:13; Deuteronomy 22:25-26

The catch phrase – a woman's right to choose – is dishonest. They don't want the little women in the womb to have their right to choose life. The little women in the womb weren't consulted before they were killed. No one asked them if they choose to give up their life. They had no say in it, no choice. What about that woman's right to choose?

The choice is not whether to have chocolate sauce on your ice cream. Abortion is serious because it results in a death – the death of a child. No one is pro-choice. Pro-choice means there's no right and wrong. It means killing a child is just as good as not killing a child. Pro-choice is a lie meant to deceive the ignorant.

Pro-choice is a trap. It implies that they are the enlightened ones who simply want women to make decisions for themselves. No. You're either for killing a baby or you're not.

Personally opposed

This is for you politicians and preachers who say you're personally opposed to abortion but support a woman's right to choose.

You're personally opposed to abortion because you know abortion is the murder of a child. You oppose murdering a child but you're for murdering a child.

The child in the womb can't hurt you. So you support killing them. That way you won't offend the women who can hurt you if you support the child's right to live.

Rape

If you're pregnant from rape and you want to know what the Bible says you should do, then I can tell you. God wants you to keep the baby, let them be born. No good can come from aborting the baby. Only bad can come from it.

Abortion doesn't heal. It's deadly serious. It's not something you want to mess with. It's too heavy. It's so awful. A little helpless baby is torn apart limb from limb. Doing that isn't going to help you. There's a better way. Turn to Jesus.   Matthew 11:28-30

And you <u>will</u> suffer negative physical and emotional reactions from the abortion. God said there are consequences for our actions. Starting on page 111, I'll show what some of those consequences are and tell you some of the reasons why God punishes people.

Don't kill the child in your womb because their father raped you.

> Do not execute a child for a crime committed by their father.
> God, Deuteronomy 24:16

Even though you went through the horror and indignity of being raped you're not given a license to kill. If that were the case then you'd be allowed to get your gun and hunt down the rapist.

What if you don't get an aborton but then two years later you decide you don't want a child that was conceived by rape? Would you have the child killed? No. But our Guide told us that a fetus is just as much a person as a two-year-old.

The child in your womb is a unique individual. You don't own that child because they're in your womb. The child belongs to God. That child comes through you, not from you. They come from God, go through you, live their life, and then they go back to God.

Ecclesiates 12:7

What's that, you say? The government legalized abortion?

Yes, they did – but God didn't. If you aborted the baby that was conceived by rape then you committed a crime as bad as rape. You murdered God's child. You're no better than the man who raped you.

> If a man rapes a woman
> then that man must be given the death penalty
> because rape is just as bad as murder.
> God, Deuteronomy 22:25-26

Some accuse God. They say that because God allowed a woman to get pregnant from rape, it means God is for rape. No, God is not for rape. God told the nation of Israel to execute rapists. God said rape was as serious a crime as murder. Some might ask, why did God let a child be conceived in the womb of a woman who was raped? Then you could ask why God allows rape and murder and all the other evil things to happen.

The Book of Job has the answer. Job was a good man who suffered the worst things that could happen to a person. Job blamed God. But then God questioned Job. God asked Job to tell Him how He created the universe and maintains it. Job couldn't answer.

When you ask why God allows evil then you're accusing God, you're calling God evil. We're in no position to do that. What we need to do is humble ourselves before God, obey Him, and trust Him. See Job 42:1-6 and Deuteronomy 32:4; Isaiah 10:33; 57:15; Micah 6:8; Luke 14:11

Have you been raped? Can I give you some advice? Don't add the words Rape Victim after your name. A lot of people have something that happened in their life. And they let it take control of the rest of their life.

Maybe when you were a child your parents divorced or one of your parents died. Maybe it was rape or another violent crime. Maybe it's an accident or a physical or intellectual disability. That doesn't have to be who you are.

And you have to pray for the man who raped you.

Yes, that's right. Forgive the man who raped you and pray for his salvation. I'm not saying don't go to the police. That's up to you. But either way, God wants you to forgive him and pray that he will be in Heaven.

You can't forgive?

Then how can you expect God to forgive you for your sins? Even if we've never raped or murdered someone we're all guilty before God. We all commit crimes deserving of death because we break God's laws. We all deserve the death penalty.   Romans 3:23; 6:23

Repent or perish.
Jesus, Luke 13:3

No, I'm not saying that getting raped is a sin. I'm not saying you got raped because you sinned. I'm saying that everyone needs Jesus. The rapist needs Jesus and the victim of rape needs Jesus.

We have to understand how holy God is. And how evil sin is. And we have to understand that the death of Jesus on the cross can pay for any sin. Even rape and murder and any other crime you can think of.

God is willing to forgive you for your sins. So how can you not be willing to forgive the man who raped you? Are you better than God? You can't ask God to forgive you for your sins but then ask God to not forgive the man who raped you. God is willing to forgive the man who raped you. If you don't forgive him then Jesus won't forgive you for your sins.   Matthew 6:14-15

If the man who raped you repents and receives Jesus then God will forgive him for raping you. If you won't repent and receive Jesus then the man who raped you will be in Heaven and you won't.

God's forgiveness is a mighty thing. God forgave king David for seducing the wife of a man named Uriah. David got her pregnant and then had Uriah killed.

When David repented God forgave David for doing those things. And God wants Uriah to forgive David.   2 Samuel 11:1-12:13

In Chapter Four I'll show you what it means to repent and be saved.

God can forgive the man who raped you. God can forgive you for your sins. And you can forgive the man who raped you. God will forgive the men who impregnated women by rape and then operated on them with no anesthetic in World War Two, if they repent and receive Jesus. I tell you this so that you will know the power that is in the death of Jesus. It can forgive and cleanse any sin.

If you aborted you're baby then you want that baby to forgive you for aborting them, right? Okay, then you have to forgive the man or men who raped you.

Why bring this up now?
You might say – don't you know that I'm a victim? Where's your compassion? Why are you saying I have to forgive the man who raped me?

I know you're a victim. But I want you to let Jesus take you from victim to victor. From victimhood to victory. There's no other remedy. There's no other way out.

I want you to turn to Jesus. When you have Jesus then you'll have the desire and ability to resist abortion and let the baby live. You'll love that baby. And whether you got pregnant or not, you'll be able to forgive and pray for the man or men who raped you. Jesus will give you truth, salvation, and peace of mind.

You can find your identity in Jesus Christ. You'll be a servant of Jesus. You won't be oppressed by something that happened to you. You'll have peace and joy in your relationship with Jesus Christ. You can go on and enjoy your life.   John 14:6

You're a man

You might be thinking – who are you to say what a woman should do, Bruce? You're a man – you can't get pregnant. You should shut up.

Really? A man can't tell a woman to let her baby live but a woman can tell the man in her womb to die?

What about the millions of men who <u>are</u> for abortion? Do you want <u>them</u> to shut up because they can't get pregnant? And what about the millions of women who oppose abortion? Will you accept what they say because they <u>can</u> get pregnant?

I was holding my Free Bible Quiz sign in Harvard Square one day and a woman came up and said – who are you to do a Bible quiz? She looked at me and decided I wasn't the one who should be doing a Bible quiz.

God gave me the ability and the right to do a Bible quiz in Harvard Square. God gives understanding to those who deserve it. And it's only those that God gives understanding to who can tell if someone else has that same understanding. The uninitiated can't.

God doesn't give someone understanding because they're a man or a woman or because they went to Bible school or because they look like a model. God looks at the heart. My being a man has nothing to do with my ability or my right to teach what the Bible says about abortion.

Truth is truth whether it's spoken by a man or a woman.

You don't go by the person. You go by what God said in the Bible. The value of the person is their ability to handle the Bible correctly. Their value is their God-given ability to teach the truth from the Bible. It's God who's talking to you then, not the person. Judge me by whether I faithfully handle the teachings in the Bible, not because I happen to be a man.

God gives understanding to both men and women.

God said men are sinning if they shut up.

Here's what God said to Ezekiel. And it applies to everyone who has God's Word, God's Holy Spirit, and His blessings, whether they're male or female.

> When I, the Lord, say the wicked will surely die,
> and you <u>don't</u> try to save their life by teaching them
> or speaking up to warn them, to try and turn them
> from their wicked way
> – and the wicked dies in their sins
> – then I will hold you guilty for their death.
>
> But if you <u>do</u> warn the wicked, and they don't turn
> from their wickedness or from their wicked ways
> – then the wicked will die in their sins.
> – but you will have saved your life.
>
> Ezekiel 3:18-19

Life of the mother

If you've ever done crossword puzzles you know that you do all the easy answers first and then work through the hard ones until you get to the hardest. We've come to the hardest.

Some of you aren't going to like my answer. If you've been looking for an excuse to fling this book across the room, here it is. Should I have avoided this question? No. I didn't need to because the answer to this question doesn't contradict or change the truth of anything I've said in this book. You can yell gotcha and call me a fraud. That's up to you. Or you can hear me out. Here's the question –

The bag of water that surrounds a child in the womb has a hole in it. The water has drained out. The baby has no chance of survival. The baby will die. The mother on the other hand, is healthy. But she too will die if the baby in her womb isn't removed. If you leave the baby to die in her womb then you sentence the mother to death. If you remove the baby then the mother lives. What do you do?

I'll answer that question in a word – intent.

The law considers intent when determining the nature of a crime and the severity of the punishment.

Abortion has one intent – to kill the child. No effort is made to preserve the child's life. An abortion has no good intent for the child being aborted. The baby has no chance. Their life has no value.

In a case like the one we're looking at now, where the bag has punctered and drained, the doctors have to perform a medical procedure. Abortion is not a medical procedure. Am I playing word games? No. The intent of a medical procedure is to save a life, not take a life.

The intent of abortion is to kill a healthy baby. When a baby has zero chance to live and their presence will kill the mother too, the intent is different. It's not the intent to kill anyone. It's a rescue mission.

What makes this case different from others?

- The baby will die if the doctors do nothing.

- The mother will die if the doctors do nothing.

- When a baby is unwanted the baby isn't dying, the baby is healthy.

- When a baby is unwanted the baby isn't going to kill their mother.

This case is different because the baby is dying. In every other case neither the baby nor the mother is dying. Most abortions are done for one reason – to get rid of an unwanted baby.

If the medical procedure is not successful and the baby dies, at least they tried to save a baby who would have died if they did nothing. A medical procedure might result in a death but it's not murder because of the intent. There's only one intent in an abortion – to end a person's life for no lawfully justifiable reason.

Doctors and families have to make difficult decisions. What if someone is brain-dead and the only reason they're alive is because of the machines they're hooked up to? The decision is made to pull the plug. The person would not go on living if they weren't hooked up to the machines. Their brain is dead. Doctors have to make decisions in a triage situation to determine which ones are more likely to live, knowing that others will die.

Why are we in this mess? Why do we have this case where a baby and their mother will die because the bag broke? Don't blame God. It wasn't this way in the Garden of Eden, the perfect place that God created. Who do we blame? The blame falls on all of us.

This all started when Adam and Eve let the devil convince them to bring sin and death into the world. The devil, Adam, and Eve let all these things into the world. So, it's because of us that this world is filled with suffering, sadness, and tragedy.

God said we're all guilty because of what Adam did. Unfair? No. And it's not an excuse for us to sin. God holds us accountable for our sins.

Romans 5:12; 6:23

Everything God does is fair and right. You have to look at the other side of the coin. God Himself came to earth and let Himself be crucified. Is that fair? God did that to take away the blame and guilt from anyone who will give their life to the Savior Jesus Christ.

Romans 5:15-21

I call the "life of the mother" argument a lying argument because it's used to deceive people. They use this rare case to argue for abortion on demand for any reason, without apology. It's a bogus kind of reasoning to use the exception to argue for the rule.

It would be like saying that because they remove a person who is brain-dead from the machine that's keeping them alive – then it's okay to kill people who are not brain-dead but who are unwanted.

The difficulty of the case at hand doesn't make abortion right or lawful. It doesn't change the fact that a fetus is a person and that abortion is the murder of a person.

Chapter Four

You've had abortions

Could God forgive you for your abortions?

There's a problem –
We break God's laws. That's called sinning. God said we must die <u>for</u> <u>our sins</u>. Abortion is sin because God's law says do not murder a person. We all die because we all commit sins like abortion. And not just our body. Our soul too must die. Jesus said that God kills both body and soul in hell.   Exodus 20:13; Matthew 10:28;
                              Romans 6:23; 1 John 3:4; Revelation 21:8

But God made a way to fix the problem.

An angel brought a message from Heaven –

> I bring good news
> to gladden your heart.
> Today in Bethlehem
> your Savior was born.
> He is the Lord, Jesus Christ.
>   Luke 2:10-11

That good news is the Gospel of Jesus Christ. The word Gospel means good news. It means you don't have to go to hell because you had abortions and I don't have to go to hell for my sins – if we believe in Jesus Christ as our Lord and Savior. So, yes, God will forgive you – if you give your life to Jesus.

The apostle Paul explains –

> I've already taught you the Gospel,
> my brothers and sisters.
> But I feel it's necessary to go over it again.
> I'll give you a simple definition
> so it will be easy for you to understand.
> When I first told you about the Gospel
> I taught you the most important things,
> exactly as Jesus taught them to me.
> I told you that Jesus Christ died <u>for our sins,</u>

just as the Old Testament said He would.
I told you that Jesus was buried,
and that He rose from the dead after three days,
just like the Old Testament said He would.

And I told you that you're saved and you'll never fall away
– if you've received and stand through
the Gospel that I've taught you.

But know also that you're <u>not</u> saved and you <u>will</u> fall away
– if you've never TRULY believed in the Gospel.
1 Corinthians 15:1-4
See Isaiah 53:9-12;
Compare Psalm 16:10 with Acts 2:25-28

I began this chapter by telling you that we all have to die <u>for our sins</u>. But Paul just said that Jesus died for our sins. You can die for your sins. Or you can let Jesus die for your sins. Jesus took the punishment you deserve. He died for your abortions so you don't have to.

Those who are found guilty will go to their punishment
with no opportunity for appeal.
But those who've been declared innocent
will go to eternal life.
Jesus, Matthew 25:46

The ones found guilty are those who rejected the Gospel of Jesus Christ. The ones declared innocent received the Gospel. Jesus makes all the difference. Paul used the word <u>saved</u>. Has anyone ever asked you if you're saved? It means you're saved from God's punishment and anger and God will welcome you to Heaven. A day will come when it will be too late. How will the people who reject the Gospel feel?

They will say to the mountains and rocks – fall on us,
and hide us from the the face of Him that sits on the throne,
and from the anger of the Lamb
because the great day of His anger has come.
Revelation 6:16-17

The Lamb is Jesus. Are you surprised to hear that Jesus feels anger? Don't you feel anger because of evil things? Jesus does too. That's how Jesus will deal with wicked people who refuse to change. Does your house have doors? Of course it does. God's house has doors too. There are some people He can't let in. Why not? Because He loves the people in His house. God doesn't want evil people coming in and hurting them.   See Mark 3:5; John 2:13-17

But if you don't want to be wicked and you have a desire to humble yourself before God and happily receive the Gospel of Jesus Christ, then you'll see a different side of Jesus –

> Come to Me, all of you who are tired out from your own effort,
> all of you who are trying to carry too much,
> and I will give you rest.
>
> Join yourself to Me
> and we will unite to become an unbreakable team.
> Let Me teach you.
> I am patient and My heart is humble.
>
> Then your soul will find the rest it was searching for.
> My friendship is always good
> and what I ask you to carry will be easy for you.
>   Jesus, Matthew 11:28-30

What is the purpose of our lives? Why are we here? Why would God put us through this? He did it to find out who loves Him. If you love God then you show your love for God by obeying Him. And our first act of obedience is when we obey the Gospel of Jesus Christ.
                              John 14:23-24; Acts 5:32; Romans 16:25-26

> The Lord Jesus will arrive from Heaven in a blazing fire.
> His mighty angels will be with Him.
> He will hand out the punishment of
> irreversible death to those who chose not to know God
> and who did not obey the Gospel of our Lord Jesus Christ.
>   2 Thessalonians 1:8-9

But that's not for you if you give your life to Jesus –

> It is not God's desire for anyone to face His anger.
> His desire is for you to obtain salvation
> through our Lord Jesus Christ, who died for us.
> 1 Thessalonians 5:9-10

Paul said you're only saved if you believe in the Gospel that he taught. Not another gospel. There's only the one Gospel.　　See Galatians 1:6-9

And Paul said you're only saved if you truly believe in Jesus. It has to be real faith. You have real faith when you repent. Repentence is the sine qua non of genuine faith. It means that repentance is the thing without which you have not. You don't have genuine faith if you don't repent. You can read the prayer of king David in Psalm 51 to see an example of genuine repentance in the Old Testament.

Titus 2:14 says Jesus gave Himself, died on a cross – in our place – to take the punishment for ALL of our sins – every one of them. Because of the death of Jesus on the cross there is not one sin that God can't forgive. The death of Jesus is powerful enough to forgive any sin. Maybe you're wondering about the "unforgivable sin." When Jesus talked about the unforgivable sin, He said –

> Anyone can have ALL of their sins forgiven.
> That's true for everyone – except for those who
> turn away from the influence of the Holy Spirit.
> They can never have forgiveness.
> They will carry the guilt of their sin until the end.
> Jesus, Mark 3:28-29

Did you read what Jesus said there? He said anyone can have all their sins forgiven. How? By going to Jesus. And WHY do we go to Jesus? Because we respond favorably to the Holy Spirit. Jesus said –

> No one can come to Me unless the Father who sent Me draws them.
> Jesus, John 6:44
> Song of Solomon 1:4; Hosea 11:2-4

When I am lifted up from the earth
I will draw everyone to Me.
Jesus, John 12:32

Lifted up from the earth means when Jesus was crucified. Drawing everyone to Him means every one of those who do give their life to Him.   See Numbers 21:8-9; John 3:14

The unforgivable sin is rejecting the Holy Spirit's power to draw you to Jesus, the Savior. Rejecting Jesus is the unforgivable sin because if you don't have Jesus then every sin is unforgivable. Abortion is not the unforgivable sin. You sinned. Don't kill yourself over it.

You're no different than anyone else. You're not special. The amazing thing is not that we sin – that's a given. The amazing thing is what God did to save us from our sins.

Every one of us are sheep who've gone astray
because we turned and went our own way.
Isaiah 53:6, and quoted in 1 Peter 2:25

Why does the death of Jesus save us?

Jesus is the propitiation for our sins.
1 John 2:2

Sorry about the big word. I wanted you to see what the King James Version calls it so you can do your own word study. It's #2434 in the Strong's Concordance. In Chapter Seven I'll show you how to do a word study. Propitiation has to do with atonement, expiation, appeasement and conciliation. More big words.

It's like if you did something that offended someone and they're angry with you. But then you find a way to fix it. You do something that makes them no longer angry with you. And instead, now they're kind, gracious, and merciful. Now they forgive you and bless you.

The Bible uses another word – reconciliation.

God reconciled us to Himself because of Jesus Christ.
2 Corinthians 5:18-19

We've all offended God by our bad behavior. God is angry with us.
Something was done to fix it. But we didn't do it. Jesus did. Jesus is
God our Savior. Jesus earned our salvation. Yes, God Himself became
a human being so He could give His life for us. Jesus took the death
you deserve for your abortions. It's called substitution.

God reconciles us to Him by the death of Jesus. Our job is to be willing
to receive that <u>reconciliation</u>. Then God is no longer angry with you.
God's justice is satisfied. Your sins are removed. Jesus paid for them
with His blood. Because of the death of Jesus our relationship with
God can be <u>restored</u>.

Does all this sound strange and scary to you? It's wonderful too. The
Old Testament tells us how God feels about those who receive the
Good News of Jesus Christ –

> None of the false gods are like You, Oh God.
> You cancel our debt of sin and remove it from our account.
> You don't stay angry forever because You delight in mercy.
> You turn to us with pity and conquer our sins,
> and send all our sins to the bottom of the sea.
> Micah 7:18-19

Do you want to reconcile with God and receive His mercy? Do you
want God to no longer be angry with you because you aborted your
baby? Do you want God to smile when He looks at you? A man came
to Paul and Silas.

The man was shaking. He fell down in front of Paul and Silas and said
what must I do to be saved?

They replied –

> Believe in the Lord Jesus Christ and you will be saved.
> Acts 16:31

Will any old believing do?
No. You need to repent. That's the opposite of rejecting the Holy
Spirit's power. God will forgive you for your abortions if you repent
and turn to Jesus. You can be 100% sure of that.

"Repent."
Jesus, Matthew 4:17

What did Jesus mean by repent? Now I'll show you an example of
genuine repentance in the New Testament. Shortly after Jesus rose
from the dead and went back to Heaven, the apostle Peter stood up
and spoke to the people. He told them that Jesus, the One they
crucified, was their Lord and Savior.   Acts 2:22-24

Some of the people in the crowd experienced a reaction when they
heard Peter tell them that. The King James Version says they were
pricked in their heart.   Acts 2:37

The word pricked is #2660 in the Strong's Concordance. It's the Greek
word katanusso. It's made up of two smaller Greek words. The first is
#2596, kata, meaning down upon. The second is the word nusso, #3572.

When Jesus was hanging on the cross, one of the Roman soldiers took
a spear and pierced Jesus in His side and immediately blood and water
came out. Pierced is that word nusso, #3572. John 19:34 (KJV).

When Peter told them they crucified their Lord and Savior the people
were pricked (nusso) in the heart. They weren't stabbed in their side
with a spear. But you could say they were stabbed in the heart.

The word nusso was used to give us an idea of how they felt when
they heard Peter tell them they crucified their Lord and Savior.

The Greek word nusso, used for the pricking of the people's hearts, is a
synonym for the Greek word ekkenteo, #1574, which is a word used
for the nailing of Jesus to the cross.   John 19:37; Revelation 1:7

What did the people hear Peter speak about?

Acts 2:11 says he spoke about the wonderful works of God (KJV). Peter spoke what Christians call God's Word. Ephesians 2:8 says we're saved by God's grace which we receive through our faith. And Romans 10:17 says faith comes by hearing God's Word. I'm feeding you God's Word. It can save your soul.

This was a special time and around 3000 people responded. Was everyone in the city pricked in the heart? No. There were many people in Jerusalem when Peter spoke. Jesus said the gate is narrow and few find it. So, if you're having a genuine conversion then you are most fortunate, indeed. Your genuine conversion makes you change your mind about abortion. Something happens that makes you know you did a terrible wrong. You admit that you're a sinner. And now you want relief.

Matthew 7:13-14; Acts 2:41

When the people were pricked in their heart they took action. They asked Peter what to do. And when Peter told them – they obeyed. This is not something you just say. It's something you do. It's a dramatic change. It's profound, deep, to your very core. The apostle Paul said he obeyed what Jesus told him to do by teaching people to repent and then live their lives in a way that people can see that they've changed.

See Luke 19:8-10; Acts 26:20

You want to repent? Think about who Jesus is and how He took action for us. Think about how much Jesus suffered – for us. Peter told the people that they crucified their Lord and Savior. Guess what. We crucified Jesus too. We put Him on that cross because of our sins. You should read Isaiah 52:13 – 53:12. And then, if you want to repent, look at Jesus on that cross –

> They will look at Him that they have pierced through,
> and they will weep uncontrollably because of Him,
> like someone weeps over the death of their only child.
> They will feel crushed over Him,
> like someone feels crushed over the death of their firstborn child.

Zechariah 12:10

Jesus was pierced with nails on the cross. And He wants you to look at Him on the cross and be pierced in your heart. You've got to humble yourself before God and then let God humble you. Jesus never sinned against God. But Jesus humbled Himself before God to teach us by His example.   See 1 Peter 2:21

Jesus humbled Himself.
Philippians 2:8

Talk to God. Tell Him how you feel. Be honest. Tell Him what you did and ask Him to forgive you. Tell Him you're sorry. That's called confessing your sin to God. If you give your life to Jesus then the promise in 1 John 1:9 is for you –

God is trustworthy and law-abiding.
If we confess our sins to Him
then He will forgive us and cleanse us
of everything that's wrong with us.
1 John 1:9

Turn from your sin and turn to Jesus with childlike faith. Be like the woman who washed the feet of Jesus with her tears.   Luke 7:36-50

Be like the person who said –

Just as the deer gasps excitedly for streams of water,
I run with breathless intensity to You, My God.
My soul thirsts for God, for the living God.
Psalm 42:1-2

The message of the Bible is resurrection from death, being reborn, new life. If you come to Jesus sincerely He won't turn you away. If you believe in Jesus with all your heart then it's over. Jesus took your guilty verdict.   See Acts 8:35-38

Repent now and turn to Jesus,
and your sins will be rubbed out.
Acts 3:19

You'll be in your right mind. Now you can claim all the promises in the Bible that God makes to believers. You can have love, joy, happiness, and peace in the Lord.   Galatians 5:22-23

> Don't have a worried mind. And don't be afraid.
> I don't give the kind of peace that this world gives.
> I give you My peace.
>   Jesus, John 14:27

> I've told you these things because I want My happiness to live in you
> – so that you'll be filled to the top with My happiness.
>   Jesus, John 15:11

1 Peter 1:8 says that those of us who have received Jesus have a happiness that cannot be described – it cannot be put into words. And we're so happy because of it that we're jumping for joy.

Jesus will welcome you with open arms. He will hug and kiss you even if you've had abortions. You can live again. He will give you His Holy Spirit. You'll be born again. You'll know you're forgiven. You'll be a new person. You'll have new thoughts and desires, and you'll live your life differently. You'll start going in the right direction.
                    John 3:3; 2 Corinthians 5:17.

When God looks at you He will see Jesus, the perfect innocence and holiness of Jesus. In God's court of law He will declare you innocent. It will be like you never had abortions –

> I will not remember your sins.
>   God, Isaiah 43:25

> There was a time when you didn't care about God.
> You made yourselves enemies of God by doing sinful things.
> But you were reconciled with God
> – because Jesus Christ lived and died in a human body.
> So that now you stand in God's presence as sinless and perfect.
> All charges against you have been dismissed.
>   Colossians 1:21-22

You're free. You won't fear God's anger and punishment anymore. It's over.

> There is therefore now no condemnation
> to them which are in Christ Jesus.
> Romans 8:1 (KJV)

Jesus said –

> Don't be afraid.
> Matthew 28:10; Mark 6:50;
> Luke 5:10; 12:7, 32;
> Revelation 1:17; 2:10; See Mark 5:36; John 12:15

One day soon you'll be in Heaven. All your bad memories will be burned up, gone forever. Jesus will personally wipe away all the tears from your eyes. Revelation 21:3-4

> Everyone who believes in Jesus
> will not be ashamed.
> Romans 10:11

Then Jesus will introduce you to the person or people you aborted. They will forgive you. They've been in Paradise enjoying pleasures beyond our ability to even imagine. You'll meet them one day and they will smile at you – the best smile you've ever seen, except for the smile you'll see on the face of Jesus. They will hug you and kiss you. All is forgiven and forgotten. We only look forward now.

Why did Jesus give His life for us?

> I am the good Shepherd.
> The good Shepherd lays down His life for the sheep.
> Jesus, John 10:11

> Laying down your life for those you love
> is the greatest act of love.
> Jesus, John 15:13

But Jesus didn't stay dead. His body was in the tomb for three days and three nights. Then Jesus rose from the dead.

Matthew 12:40; 28:5-6; Mark 8:31; John 2:19-21

Don't be afraid. I am the First and the Last.
I am Life, but I became dead.
Now look! I'm alive.
Yes, I'm the One who gives eternal life forever and ever.

Jesus, Revelation 1:17-18

We have happiness with God because of Jesus Christ.

Romans 5:11

What if you're a Christian and you engaged in sexual immorality and got sexually transmitted diseases (STDs)? God will forgive you for your sexual immorality but your body might suffer pain or even death from those sexully transmitted diseases. What if you're a Christian and you had an abortion? God will forgive you for having an abortion but your body might react to the abortion by getting breast cancer

If our sins had no negative consequences we would have no reason to stop doing them. We might get STDs from sexually immorality, or breast cancer from having an abortion because God wants our sins to have consequences. God wants us to know that sin is a serious matter. Look at what Jesus went through to pay the penalty for our sins.

Matthew 26:65-68; Mark 15:15-20

Get on your knees and thank God for the illness you got from your sins. Your pain will make you more serious about devoting your life to working for Jesus.

See Hebrews12:6

> Always have a spirit of thankfulness
> because you belong to Jesus Christ
> – no matter what happens to you.

> And then, when God sees you do that,
> it will make Him happy.
> 1 Thessalonians 5:18

You're reading this book, so you're alive. Make the most of what you have. Use what God gives you in the place He puts you. Serve God and have contentment. Always be thankful because of Jesus.

God is so amazing. He can do anything. There's something He does for those who love Him because He loves us so much.

Here's a Bible verse that people misuse –

> And we know that all things work together for good
> to them that love God.
> Romans 8:28 (KJV)

Do you look to the cross of Christ? Are you pricked in your heart? Do you cry over your sins? Do you turn to Jesus in humble obedience? No? Then you don't love God. And if you think this verse applies to you then you're misusing this verse. Jesus said if you're not obeying Him then you don't love Him.   John 14:15,21,23-24

But if you do truly love God then you can put your trust in the promise God made in that verse. It's for you.

Do you feel weak?

The apostle Paul said

> I'm strong when I'm weak.
> God told me His power works best in weakness.
> 2 Corinthians 12:9-10

> My grace is enough strength for you.
> God, 2 Corinthians 12:9

When we're weak, when we let God humble us, when we're not filled with stubborn pride – then God can use us.

Maybe you're a Christian and you had abortions and you repented and asked God to forgive you – you know He forgives you – but you still feel bad. Sometimes I wake up in the morning and think about the bad way I treated my parents and other people. I remember things I did when I was six years old. My street preacher friend Tilman Gandy said God will forgive but the central nervous system might not.

Sometimes we start thinking about sins we've committed and worry if God really could forgive us for doing such evil things. We don't want to do that. It's like calling God a liar. We know that God can and does forgive the sins of those who love Him. He wipes the slate clean

If you're shocked that you had an abortion then you're thinking too highly of yourself. We're human. We all sin horribly. That's what humans do.

We look back at things we did and can't believe we did them. We're shocked, ashamed, and disgusted. Use that as a lesson. It's only by an act of God that we're able to do good. Everybody sins. Christians sin.

If the death of Jesus couldn't pay for every sin then we would all be doomed.

When I start feeling bad or thinking about something I did in the past, wondering if God could possibly forgive me for it, I ask God to forgive me for doubting His forgiveness and thinking the sacrifice of Jesus on the cross didn't work. Then I say the name Jesus out loud and I say peace and joy in the Lord.

> God doesn't give us a fearful mind.
> He gives us His power and love
> so we can have a disciplined mind.
> 2 Timothy 1:7

Know that your future is in Heaven. And because you've received Jesus, you can do this –

> Here's what you can do once and for all
> with those worries that are eating you up.
> Grab hold of all of them. Get a good tight grip.
>
> Now throw them as hard as you can.
> Throw them on God. Yes, you can do that.
>
> Why? Because God is concerned about you.
> 1 Peter 5:7

I have something to tell you
If I could say one thing to anyone, whether they're a Christian or not, this is it. It's the most urgent issue of our time. It will determine whether you succeed or fail, whether you have peace or anxiety, whether you have truth or error.

And it's this – you have to study the Bible.

What is the greatest evil?
It's when the Bible is taken from people or when people who have the Bible choose to ignore it.

I said this same thing to hundreds of people at my street ministry. No matter what ailment they complained of, I always prescribed the same medicine – study the Bible. Many responded by saying – oh, I can't do that. Well, then you're gonna have problems.

Whether or not you acquire a taste for Bible study is between you and God, just like your salvation is between you and God. I can't give you either of them. All I can do is tell you that a taste for Bible study is the best thing. You might believe me or you might not. I hope you do.

If you knew what you're missing you'd get on your knees every day and plead with God to give you a taste for Bible study. Of course, one reason you don't have a taste for it is because you rarely open your Bible.

And I'm talking to fellow Christians too. I've been to churches. I know that most Christians don't study the Bible, don't know how to study, and have no idea what they're missing. A lot of Christians think they study the Bible but they really don't.

When you find out what you missed then you'll cry from regret.

If you're a Christian and you don't study the Bible then what good are you? You won't have wisdom and discernment. You won't be blessed by God. Lack of Bible study is the biggest problem in the world. Because of it the devil and his ministers are getting away with murder.

I'm not just telling you to study the Bible, I'm showing you how to study. Open your Bible and use your mind. Use your imagination. Think of ways to share with people what you learn from your Bible study.

God gave me the idea of creating interesting questions that teach a truth from the Bible. That's how I started my street ministry.

I'll tell you from my own experience
If you want to be blessed then you need to do intense Bible study. It has to be your greatest love. It has to be first in your life. You've got to have your mind in the Bible throughout your day. This is not a hobby. You don't read from a devotional in the morning like it's a cup of coffee.

Be like a football coach who's trying to win a championship. Be like the people who send a ship to Mars. You have to be immersed, absorbed, saturated. Yes, of course, you have your job and family. Of course you give them their proper consideration.

But your Bible study is even more important. It's your first love. Your job and family will pass away. But your Bible study gives you treasures in Heaven that never pass away. Keep your mind in the Bible. Be in the Word.

The Bible is the most valuable, most precious thing in the world.

After you receive Jesus you'll still experience suffering. That's because we live in a world that's been corrupted by sin. And we live in bodies made of flesh that are subject to temptation, sickness, and death. And genuine Christians are hated by the world.

But you'll have moments of intense joy. You'll be focused on the work God gives you to do. And you'll have the sure promise of living with Jesus in Heaven forever. The day will come when Jesus will put us in our eternal, sinless, spiritual bodies.   Revelation 21:3-4

> Receive the helmet of salvation
> and the sword of the Spirit, which is the Word of God.
>
> Pray in the Spirit through everything that comes at you.
> Talk to God and tell Him what you need.
>
> Be ready. Be serious, unwavering, unflinching, unmovable.
> And pray for the needs of your Christian brothers and sisters.
> Ephesians 6:17-18

Some people tell you they're Christians.
Then they say the Bible has no problem with abortion.

Do you know how to respond?
In chapters five to ten I'll show you how.

Chapter Five

Breath or blood?

"Choose life"
God, Deuteronomy 30:19

Does a fetus breathe?

Here's a lying argument made by people who call themselves
Christians. They claim they learned this one from the Bible.

They say the Bible teaches that a person's life is in their breath – and
therefore a fetus is not alive until it's born and takes its first breath.
They conclude then that God has no problem with abortion.

Really? You can't tell by simple observation that there's a living child
in the womb?

In the debate over abortion it doesn't matter where our life is, and it
doesn't matter if a fetus breathes or doesn't breathe. We know the
truth. Our Guide already told us. A fetus is a person.

Yes, there are verses that seem to say our life is in our breath. And
there are verses that more emphatically say our life is in our blood.
But guess what, a child in the womb has both breath and blood.

Does a fetus breathe?
The lungs of a child in the womb are filled with water. They don't
breathe through their lungs. When they're born then they cry and gasp
and take their first breath as the water leaves their lungs.

But you're mistaken if you think that means a fetus doesn't breathe.
The child in the womb does breathe – in a different way. The fetus
lives in their mother's uterus. The uterus is also called the womb.
When a woman becomes pregnant an organ called the placenta grows
in her uterus. The placenta is connected to the child by a cord called
the umbilical cord.

The child receives from their mother everything their body needs to
live. The mother breathes air through her lungs for her child and eats
solid food for her child. The mother sends food, blood, and oxygen to
the baby in her womb. They're carried through the blood in the
umbilical cord and go into the child's heart and bloodstream.

Then the child sends urine and carbon dioxide back through the umbilical cord to the mother and her body disposes of them. So, the baby does breathe because of the oxygen that flows from the mother into the placenta, then through the umbilical cord to the baby.

So, we know those Christians came to the wrong conclusion. And we know that the Bible never says it's okay to kill a fetus.

Here's a short Bible study on the subject of breath and blood. I gave several examples about breath. Please don't leave me. Enjoy them.

• Genesis 2:7 is a favorite verse for those who make the false claim that a fetus isn't a person until they're born and take their first breath.

> The Lord God formed Adam out of the dust of the ground,
> and breathed the breath of life into his nostrils,
> and Adam became a living person.
> Genesis 2:7

The first thing you need to know is that Adam was an exception. Adam never saw the inside of a womb – he didn't have a mother. So God had to do something special for him.

Did God do mouth-to-mouth resuscitation on Adam? Or was it a spiritual breathing? The Bible uses breath, air, and wind to symbolize spiritual things.

• A man named Nicodemus came to meet Jesus and Jesus told him that a person can't go to Heaven if they don't have a second birth – if they're not born again by the Spirit, God's Holy Spirit.   John 3:1-5

Then, Jesus said –

> The WIND goes wherever it wants to. You can hear the sound the wind makes – but you can't see the place where it came from and you don't know where it will go. And that's how it is with everyone who receives a second birth from the SPIRIT.
> Jesus, John 3:8

In John 3:8, the words wind and Spirit are both the same word in the original Greek – pneuma, #4151. The wind is physical and God's Holy Spirit is spiritual. But the same Greek word is used for both.

• In the King James Version, 2 Timothy 3:16 says that every word of the Bible was "given by inspiration of God." The original Greek uses just one word, theopneustos, #2315. You can see Theo in that word. That's the word God in Greek, #2316. And there's pneustos. It looks like pneuma, the word in John 3:8 that was used for both the wind and God's Spirit. That's because they're of the same family. See #4154.

The literal meaning of 2 Timothy 3:16 in the original Greek is that God breathed every word of the Bible into the men who wrote them down. Did God breathe the words physically or spiritually?

• In John 20:22, Jesus breathed on His disciples and said – receive the Holy Spirit.

• In Ezekiel, chapter 37, God breathed life into dry bones. It means God breathed His Holy Spirit into people who'd been starved to death spiritually by bad pastors who didn't feed them God's Word.

Verses in the Bible that seem to say our life is in our breath –

• When the prophet Elijah was homeless and hungry God told him to go to a woman in Zarepheth. God told Elijah that He instructed the heart of that woman to feed him. While Elijah was there the woman's son died. The Bible doesn't say he died. It says there was no breath left in him.   1 Kings 17:17

• Job said –

> I will not speak wickedness or deceit
> all the while my breath is in me.
> Job 27:3-4

By "all the while my breath is in me" Job meant his whole life.

• God made a flood and saved only Noah and his family. After it was all over, Genesis 7:22 says that all who had the breath of life in their nostrils had died. So, it sounds like they lost their life when they lost the ability to breathe.

• Joshua 11:14 says that Israel did as God commanded them and did not leave any to breathe. So breathing is the opposite of being dead.

How is blood different?

I would say that when the Bible talks about life being in the breath it's more of a symbolic thing. The Bible speaks of life being in the blood in a more literal way. God didn't say the words, "the life of the flesh is in the <u>breath</u>." But God did say this –

> The life of the flesh is in the <u>blood</u>.
> God, Leviticus 17:11

All four Gospels record the death of Jesus. Instead of saying Jesus died all four Gospels say Jesus gave up the ghost. The word ghost is that Greek word pneuma, #4151, that can mean wind, breath, spirit, or Spirit. Does that mean then that the life in the body of Jesus was in His breath?

> "Gave up the ghost" is in Matthew 27:50;
> Mark 15:37; Luke 23:46 and John 19:30

On the night before Jesus would die by crucifixion He met with His apostles. Jesus took a cup, gave thanks for it, and handed it to the apostles. Jesus said drink from it, all of you – because this is My blood of the new covenant – which will be shed for many as the payment for their sins.   Matthew 26:27-28; See John 19:2, a crown of thorns

Jesus didn't say take this cup, all of you, and breathe. Jesus didn't say this is My breath. He said this is My blood that is given for you. When Jesus said My blood, He meant My death. Romans 3:25 says we're saved by faith in His blood. They didn't kill Jesus by squeezing the breath out of Him. Jesus wasn't strangled or smothered. Jesus was whipped brutally. They put a crown of thorns on His head. Jesus bled.

When the crowd insisted that Jesus be crucified, Pontius Pilate washed his hands and said, I am innocent of the blood of this just Person. He meant he was innocent for the death of Jesus.   Matthew 27:24 KJV

In the Bible murder is not called the shedding of breath. Murder is called the shedding of blood. The word is bloodshed, not breathshed. God didn't say murderers have breath on their hands. No one faints at the sight of breath.   Genesis 9:6; Ezekiel 23:45

I hope you enjoyed that Bible study.

Don't believe people who says it's okay to kill a child because they haven't yet breathed through their lungs. They're deceiving you. Beware of anyone who tells you they're a Christian and who makes that argument. They want to feed you through an unbiblical cord.

They're one of the wolves in sheep's clothing that Jesus warned us about.   Matthew 7:15-23; See Acts 20:29-31

In Titus 1:9-11, the apostle Paul warned that deception will come from people who call themselves Christians. Paul said they're like people who pretend to be your friend and then stab you in the back. They use words like Bible and Christian. They speak with authority. But they hate the truth from the Bible.

• Paul said their teachings are not sound teachings. (Paul used a Greek word for sound that means healthy. Sound teachings are teachings that are true, pure, whole, and give spiritual health).

• Paul calls them deceivers. The Greek word is phrenapates, #5423. It's made up of two words. The first part is phren, #5424. It means your mind. The second part is apate, #539, which comes from apateo, #538. It means to deceive or to cheat. They deceive your mind. They're smooth talking con men and women who cheat you out of the truth.

• Paul said it's the job of genuine Christians to silence those imposters. Paul used a word that means to muzzle the mouth of an animal to stop them from biting people.   Titus 1:11

We do that by giving people the healthy teachings. We give people the pure Word of God. And God's Holy Spirit will take care of it.

Paul and Silas went to Berea and taught the people. And the people examined the Bible every day. Why? To see if what Paul and Silas were teaching matched up with what the Bible says. When someone tells you they're a Christian and they say that God has no problem with abortion, then you have to examine the Bible to see if what they teach matches up with what the Bible teaches.   See Acts 17:10-12

Whether you believe our life is in our breath or our blood, one thing is sure. It's a bogus argument to say abortion is okay because life might begin at breath. It's evil math. The Bible says a fetus is a person.

You would have to willfully close your eyes to not know that a fetus is a child. The fetus is a living person until you kill them by abortion.

The living spirit that God put in the fetus is in the blood flowing through their veins.Their life drains out when they bleed to death during the abortion.

Chapter Six

Christian liberty

Did Jesus give Christians free will to have abortions?

I have a question for the people who say Jesus gave them free will to
have an abortion. Where do you get your information? Because there's
no such thing in the Bible as the free will to kill a child.

Jesus said this to some who spoke falsely –

> The reason you're deceived is that you
> don't know the Bible or the power of God.
> Jesus, Matthew 22:29

You might be thinking – oh sure Bruce, you know the answers because
you're some kind of scholar. No. I've never set foot in a university.
Actually, you need just two things to find the answers in the Bible –
God's blessings and hard work.

> Deuteronomy 6:6-9; Matthew 16:17;
> Acts 17:11; 2 Timothy 2:15; Hebrews 11:6

There's a Greek word used in the New Testament for will, as in free
will. It's thelema, #2307 in the Strong's Concordance.

What does the Bible say about a Christian's free will?
In Luke 11:1, one of the disciples of Jesus said, Lord, teach us how to
pray. And Jesus told the disciples that when they pray to God, to say –

> "Your will (thelema) be done."
> Luke 11:2

In Revelation 4:11, the King James Version says that God created
everything for His "pleasure." The word "pleasure" is the Greek word
thelema.

In Matthew 12:50, Jesus said – who is My brother, and sister, and
mother? It's whoever does the will (thelema) of My Father, God. Jesus
said it like that to show how dear they are to Him – those who choose
to obey God and do what pleases Him.

Jesus said you won't go to Heaven just because you call yourself a Christian. Jesus said the only ones who go to Heaven are the ones who do the will (thelema) of <u>God</u>.

Matthew 7:21

Jesus did made Christians free, 2 Corinthians 3:17; 1 Peter 2:16. The Bible calls it Christian liberty. Do the math –

• What is Christian liberty? Jesus told us –

> Listen to what I'm about to say. If you decide to make
> sin your daily routine, then you'll be the slave of sin.
> I'll say it again. If you give yourself over to sin
> then you'll truly be the slave of sin.
> But if I make you free, then you'll be truly free.
> Jesus, John 8:34,36

Jesus said Christian liberty is freedom from slavery to sin.

• What is sin?

Sin is the breaking of God's law.   1 John 3:4.

• Is abortion against God's law?

Thou shall not murder a person. Exodus 20:13.

Yes, abortion is against God's law. Abortion is sin. Sin is not a Christian liberty. It's not God's will for Christians to sin. Therefore, calling abortion a Christian liberty is bad math.

• Who has Christian liberty?

> When you allow yourself to obey someone
> as though you were their slave – then you are their slave.
> You can be an obedient slave to sin, which will kill you.
> Or you can be an obedient slave to righteousness.

But thank God that you who were the slaves of sin
made the decision to be obedient
and follow the pattern of teachings that were given to you.
So now you've been made free from sin's power to enslave you.
And instead, you've become slaves
to the righteousness of God.
Romans 6:16-18

Only those who obey Christ have Christian liberty.

• What did Jesus do to give us that liberty?

The children of Jesus live in a human body.
That's why Jesus came and lived in a human body too.
Jesus did that so He could die.
Because when Jesus died He took away the devil's ability
to use death as a weapon against His children.
The devil had been holding the children of Jesus in slavery to the
fear of death for their whole lives.
But when Jesus died He set His children free.
Hebrews 2:14-15

Christian liberty means Christians can confess our sins to God in the
name of Jesus Christ and be forgiven because Jesus paid the penalty
for our sins by dying on the cross. It means we don't have to live in
fear of death and the devil. The devil has no legal case against us. It
means that now we can obey God's law. We can become slaves of
Christ instead of slaves to sin. Now that's Christian liberty! Thank you
Jesus! 1 Peter 2:16

A warning from Jesus –

When the king came in to look closely at the guests
he noticed one who did not have on a wedding garment.
And the king said to them, Excuse me, pal,
how did you get in here without a wedding garment?
And the person said nothing.
So the king said to his helpers,

Tie this person's hands and feet together.
Now pick them up and throw them out of here
and into the darkness
– where there will be weeping and gnashing of teeth.
Jesus, Matthew 22:11-13

That's the conclusion of a story Jesus told about a wedding feast. The wedding feast is to celebrate the wedding of Jesus with His genuine followers. The person who snuck in without a wedding garment is someone pretending to be a genuine follower of Jesus.　See Isaiah 54:5

There are many, many people who tell you they're a Christian – but they're imposters. They don't have on a wedding garment. Instead they have on sheep's clothing. They wear that to make you think they're a Christian. But they're wolves disguised as sheep. It's the oldest trick in the book. It's what the devil did to Eve. But they won't fool Jesus. And Jesus doesn't want His followers to be deceived by them.　　　　　Genesis 3:1-19; Matthew 7:15-27; 24:3-4;
Acts 20:28-31; 2 Corinthians 11:14-15; 1 John 4:1; Jude 1:3-4

The Bible says abortion is murder. So, people call themselves Christians and create a New Christianity that supports their sinful desires. Their New Christianity calls abortion a blessing. They have their own Jesus and their own gospel. The New Christianity is fake and deadly.

That's why Christians must study the Bible. Then we'll be able to use the sword of the Spirit, which is the Word of God.　　　Ephesians 6:17

I didn't just blurt out an answer. I took you into the Bible. The next time someone says Jesus gives Christians free will to have an abortion, ask them to prove it from the Bible. And let me know what they say, please.

If you continue in My Word then you are My true disciples,
and you will know the truth, and the truth will set you free.
Jesus, John 8:31-32

Chapter Seven

Is there a passage in the Bible that okays abortion?

Exodus 21:22-25

The Bloodyhands say this is where God gave them permission to do abortions.

Exodus 21:22-25 deals with a case where men are fighting and they accidentally hit a pregnant woman.

The argument comes down to one word in verse 22 – "depart," #3318. Some Bible versions translate it as a miscarriage – that when the men hit the woman she had a miscarriage and the baby died. Other Bible versions say the baby was born prematurely – but the baby survived.

Verse 22 also says that if no further harm is done then the men who hit the woman must pay a fine. The Bloodyhands like the Bible versions that say the baby is dead. That way, when the verse says if no further harm is done, it has to refer to the mother. That would mean the fine is paid for the death of the fetus.

The Bible says the punishment for murdering a person is death. The Bloodyhands say that here, in verse 22, the killing of the fetus is only punished by a fine. So, they conclude that God doesn't think a fetus is as valuable as an adult. Then they take it another step and claim that God is saying it's okay to abort fetuses.

Here's what's wrong with that argument –

Governments have laws against first degree murder, second degree murder, and manslaughter. In all three a person is dead. But the penalty is less for manslaughter than for first degree murder. That doesn't mean the person killed by manslaughter had less value than the person killed by first degree murder. The law considers the intent of the guilty person, not the value of the person who was killed. This principle comes from the Bible.   Exodus 21:12-14; Deuteronomy 19:4-7

So, even if it were true that the baby died and the penalty was a fine, it wouldn't mean the baby's life was less valuable than an adult's life. But this passage does not say that a fine is paid if the fetus dies.

God gives people free will. People can write anything and call it a Bible version. Don't assume it must be right because it calls itself the Bible.

One Bible version says one thing and another says the opposite. We're not Hebrew scholars – what do we do? What we do is we get the truth directly from God. How do we do that? By studying the Bible. Jesus said ask, seek, knock – and you will find – Luke 11:9-10. Show God that you're serious, that you're willing to do your part, do the work, and make the effort. If you do that then God will reward you.

I told you something in my book – Jehovah's Witnesses hate Jehovah. And I'm telling you again. Find the context. Here's the context to interpret Exodus 21:22 correctly. From Genesis to Psalms to Matthew and Luke, God told us that a fetus is a person. God is not going to then turn around and tell us in in Exodus 21:22-25 that a fetus has little value and that He's okay with abortion.

Our Guide taught us that a fetus is a person from conception – with the same right to live – 100% as valuable as anyone who's been born. God said so. That's the truth. So, the Bloodyhands argument is a lie. Now you know. God did not say abortion is okay. But you need to know more. Now I'm going to show you how to study the Bible. Here's Exodus 21:22 in the King James Version –

If men strive, and hurt a woman with child, so that her fruit depart from her, and yet no mischief follow: he shall surely be punished, according as the woman's husband will lay upon him; and he shall pay as the judges determine.   Exodus 21:22 (KJV)

The Bible sometimes calls children fruit.

What did I do when I came to this passage in Exodus 21:22-25?

First, I read interpretations, commentaries, and articles written by both the Bloodyhands and the Speakfors. Jesus used that method. Jesus taught the people by showing them the differences between the false teachings of the Pharisees and God's teachings.

You can see that in the Sermon on the Mount in Matthew 5:1 to 7:29, and in other teachings of Jesus throughout the four Gospels.

Matthew 21:33-46; 23:1-39; Luke 16:19-31

By reading those commentaries and articles I got an idea of the arguments by both sides. And I got ideas about other passages in the Bible that will help me understand this one.

Then I looked up all the words in verse 22 in the original Hebrew. What is the original Hebrew for child and – her fruit depart – and mischief? Yes – you. You must do that. Don't let anyone tell you that you can't. If you're a Christian then the Holy Spirit will Guide you.

This passage is in the Old Testament so that means it was originally written in Hebrew. I use the King James Version because it's the version used by most of the books that are available to study the meanings of words in the original languages. Here's what you do.

The first part – if men strive, means if men fight, violently, punching each other. Then they hurt a woman with child. You can look up the word hurt in the Strong's Concordance. Then you go down the list and find the verse, Exodus 21:22. Then there's a number for hurt, #5062.

Now you go to the Hebrew dictionary in the back of the Strong's Concordance and see what the word meant in the original Hebrew. Then you can take that same number, 5062, and study its Hebrew meaning in the Brown – Driver – Briggs Hebrew and English Lexicon. And that number is also used in The Complete Word Study Dictionary of the Old Testament, Warren Baker, D.R.E., Eugene Carpenter, Ph.D.

In this passage the word means to hit. The men who were fighting accidentally bumped into or accidentally punched a woman with child. What's a woman with child?

You know what a woman is. But what does this verse mean by child? The number for child is 2030. It means the woman in Exodus 21:22 has conceived a child in her womb. I want to dig into the Bible to get more understanding of what's meant here by child.

So I take another book off the shelf. It's called The Englishman's Hebrew Concordance of the Old Testament, George V. Wigram. This book also uses the numbers from the Strong's Concordance. I look up the word for child, #2030, in the verse we're studying, Exodus 21:22.

This book shows me all the places where that Hebrew word is used in the Old Testament. I counted fifteen. One of the places the word appears is Isaiah 7:14, which predicts that Mary, the virgin, will conceive a Child in her womb. Matthew 1:23 tells us that the Child is Jesus. The first place the word is used is in Genesis 16:11, when the Angel of the Lord told Hagar that she was with child. That child was born and named Ishmael.

You can go down the list and look at all fifteen. It's obvious what the word means. It means a child.

> Genesis 16:11; 38:24,25; Exodus 21:22;
> Judges 13:5,7; 1 Samuel 4:19; 2 Samuel 11:5;
> 2 Kings 8:12; 15:16; Isaiah 7:14; 26:17; Jeremiah 20:17: 31:8; Amos 1:13

The next thing we read in Exodus 21:22 is that the men who were fighting bumped the pregnant woman so hard that it caused her fruit to depart from her. The word fruit is # 3206, and it means a child. The Bible calls a child the fruit of the womb. A womb produces a child just like a fruit tree produces fruit. Fruit means results.

In our verse, the word depart, #3318, means comes out. This is the word the Bloodyhands claim means the baby died. But the word is used in Genesis 25:26 when Jacob came out of his mother Rebekah's womb when he was born – alive. And #3318, came out , is used in Genesis 38:28-30 to say that Pharez and Zarah were born – alive.

When a woman miscarries the baby dies. The Bible has a word for miscarriage. In Exodus 23:26 God told the children of Israel that if they obey Him then none of their women will cast their young (KJV). The expression cast their young is # 7921. It means to miscarry (Hosea 9:14). If God had been talking about miscarriage in Exodus 21:22, as the Bloodyhands claim, then He would have used # 7921, the word for miscarriage. He didn't. He used a word that simply means came out.

There's another word used for a baby that's born dead. It's #5309. It's used in Job 3:16; Psalm 58:8, and Ecclesiastes 6:3. God didn't use that word either in the passage we're studying, Exodus 21:22. God used #3318, the word used for a baby who is born alive.

So, Exodus 21:22 is talking about a child that came out prematurely because their mother was bumped. It is not talking about a miscarriage. The men bump the woman and the child comes out of her womb. And then we read – and yet no mischief follow. What's mischief? It means damage or harm, #611. So the baby comes out but the baby is not harmed, the baby survives because there's no mischief. In that case the men who were fighting have to pay a fine to compensate the woman and her husband for causing the baby to come out prematurely.

In the next verses, Exodus 21:23-25, we're told what happens to the men who bumped the woman if mischief does follow. They must give life for life, or eye for eye, or tooth for tooth, etc. If bumping the woman caused the baby who came out to die then the men must also die. They are guilty of murder. If the baby lost an eye then they must lose an eye.

So, What does Exodus 21:22-25 say should happen if men have a fist fight and bump a pregnant woman?

• If the child comes out, is born prematurely, and the child lives, and there's no serious harm done to the child – and the mother lives and there's no serious harm done to the mother – then the men who bumped into the woman must pay a fine to the women's family.

• But if either the child or the mother dies, then the men who bumped them must pay with their life. And if either the child or mother lost an eye or a tooth, etc., then the men who bumped them must lose an eye or a tooth, etc.

God called for the execution of men who caused the death of a baby in the womb because of their careless mischief. How do you think God feels about the slaughter of children going on in the world today?

Numbers 5:11-31

The Bloodyhands claim that in Numbers 5:11-31, a pregnant woman, her husband, and a priest met together and decided that the woman should have an abortion. So, they say, it means that God is okay with a pregnant woman, her husband, and her doctor meeting to decide that the woman should have an abortion. That's a lie. I'll make this easy –

In Numbers 5:11-31, God told the nation of Israel what to do if a man was jealous because his wife had sex with another man.

The Bloodyhands case rests on the punishment inflicted on the wife if she's found guilty. This is found in verse 21 and repeated in verse 22. The King James Version says her thigh will rot and her belly will swell. The Bloodyhands prefer the Bible versions that say she will miscarry. Then they say, see, that's an abortion. And then they claim it means that God permits abortion.

No. In the first verses of the passage, Numbers 5:11-12, God spoke to Moses and told Moses to explain this ritual to the people. In verse 16 we're told that the priest is supposed to set the woman before the Lord. So, God Himself is going to be the Witness, the Judge, and the one who carries out the punishment. God decides what happens to the woman, not the woman, her husband, or the priest.

Even if the woman was pregnant and her baby died – it was God who killed the baby. That means there's no case to be made for abortion from this ritual.

God said YOU shall not murder a person. It's not murder when God kills someone. God can kill a child – you can't. When you abort children you're playing God. When you abort a baby you're committing murder – a most evil murder.

What happened when king David seduced a man's wife and she got pregnant? God killed the newborn child. The Bloodyhands could say that means God is okay with them killing newborn children.

See 2 Samuel 12:13-19

Chapter Eight

The consequences

"Holy, holy, holy, Lord God Almighty"
Revelation 4:8 (KJV)

How does God feel about abortion?

How does God feel about children being thrown in the trash with the coffee grounds? What do you think?

In the Old Testament God warned over and over not to kill innocent people. And God explained in vivid detail the terrifying punishments waiting for those who kill the innocent. Children are innocent. They've done nothing to deserve death.

> I hate people who shed innocent blood. They make Me sick.
> God, Proverbs 6:16-17

The Bloodyhands are like the people who wanted Jesus dead even though Jesus was innocent. The Roman leader Pontius Pilate was someone who killed easily. But he told the people that he questioned Jesus and couldn't find any reason to kill Him.

> Matthew 27:11-26; Luke 13:1

The people didn't care. They said – crucify Him anyway! So Pilate agreed to crucify Jesus. But first, Pilate did a symbolic act – and he wanted the people to see it. In front of everyone he washed his hands with water. Then he told them – I won't take the blame for the blood of this law-abiding Man. You take it.

> They can't wait to shed innocent blood.
> Isaiah 59:7

And the people said – let His blood be on us. The blood of Jesus that Pilate said he wouldn't take the blame for, is the death of Jesus. When the people said let His blood be on us, the word blood means the guilt for the death of Jesus.

The blood of aborted children is on the Bloodyhands.

> I'll hold you guilty if you kill an innocent person.
> God, Exodus 23:7

> I have sinned because I delivered
> innocent blood to a death sentence.
> Judas Iscariot, Matthew 27:4

God gave governments the authority to kill people. Murder is so serious that God said a person who commits murder must be killed by the government. But governments must never kill innocent people.

Genesis 9:5-6

God reserves a special punishment for a nation that murders their children –

> I'll make bad things happen to those who
> take money to kill innocent people.
> God, Deuteronomy 27:25

Then God followed that up in Deuteronomy 28:53-57 by giving a detailed account of the bad things that will happen to a nation that makes it their business to kill innocent children –

> Every city and town will be shut down by your enemies
> – a lockdown so bad you'll resort to violence to survive.
> You'll eat the flesh of your sons and daughters,
> which the Lord your God has given you.
>
> A man who is well-bred and soft-hearted
> will become cold-blooded toward his brother
> and toward his beloved wife and toward the children
> that he hasn't eaten,
>
> so that he will not share with any of them
> the flesh of his children that he does eat,
> – because he has nothing else to eat.
>
> The woman who is refined and elegant
> – a woman so pampered and dainty that she wouldn't
> so much as set the sole of her foot upon the ground

– she will be brutal to her dear husband
and to her sons and her daughters.

She will eat them because of her lack of all things.
She will hide somewhere and eat them
because of the anguish during the shutdown
that your enemies will force on you in all your cities.
God, Deuteronomy 28:53-57

And many years later it happened as God said it would. One day, a
woman cried out to the king of Israel, Jehoram, asking him to help her.
The king asked her what was wrong. And she said her friend told her –
if you give your son today so we can eat him, then I'll give my son for
us to eat tomorrow.

The woman told the king that she did as her friend said. They boiled
her son and ate him. But the next day,when she said to her friend –
give your son now so we can eat him – her friend had hidden her son.
You can read that in 2 Kings 6:26-30.

You might say that was just for Israel, or, that's the Old Testament. No,
you're wrong. The principle applies to every nation. Do you think God
only told Israel not to kill children but it's okay for other nations to?
No. Never.

God told Israel what He would let happen to them if they reject His
laws. And God deals the same way with people who don't have Moses
and don't have the Bible but who reject His laws and do these things.
I'll tell you in a second what these things are –

Don't pollute yourselves in any of these things.
I'm kicking out the nations who do these things.
I'm getting them out of your face
because they polluted themselves by doing all these things.

Because of them the land itself became polluted.
And I told the land that it was guilty and to do something about it.
So the land vomitted out its inhabitants.

You must keep My rules and regulations
and watch over My Divine Law.
And you must not do any of these disgusting things.
so that the land doesn't vomit you out too.
Leviticus 18:24-28

Yes, the land suffers too because of our sins. See Genesis 3:17 and
Romans 8:19-22. So, what are these things, these disgusting things?
They're listed in Leviticus 18:6-23. The one we're dealing with now is –

You shall not give your children over to Molech.
Leviticus 18:21

The nations God punished were the Canaanite nations. They weren't
Israel. The land God was talking about is Canaan, also known as the
Promised Land. Molech was an idol, a false god that the Canaanites
worshiped. Israel copied the Canaanites and burned their children to
death as sacrifices to Molech –

They killed their sons and daughters as sacrifices to demons.
They shed innocent blood – the blood of their sons and daughters
when they sacrificed them to the idols of Canaan
and the land was polluted with blood.
Psalm 106:37-38

Before the children of Israel went into Canaan, the Promised Land,
God gave them another warning –

When you go into the land that the Lord God has given you
then you must always obey Me.
Don't ask about the gods of the people who were there before you.
Don't start thinking that you should do
what they did to serve their gods.
You must never do for Me what they did for their gods.
Because every disgusting thing that I hate
is what they did for their gods.
They even burned their sons and daughters
in fire to serve their gods.   – God, Deuteronomy 12:1,30-31

I wanted to show you that when God said they gave their children over to Molech in Leviticus 18:21, what He meant is that they burned their sons and daughters to death as sacrifices in idol worship to the false god Molech. I said idol worship, and maybe you want to say to me –

"Abortion isn't idol worship, Bruce – we're not sacrificing to Molech."

No. You're wrong. Abortion is idol worship. Getting free of that child is your idol. You obey that idol instead of obeying God. The Bible says greed is idol worship.

Ephesians 5:5; Colossians 3:5;
See 1 Samuel 15:23; Ezekiel 14:1-7; 1 John 2:15; 5:21

Did you have an abortion because spending money on the child would have meant having less money for your drug habit? Did you have an abortion because a child would intefere with your education or your career? Or did you have an abortion because you didn't want to be burdened with a baby? Matthew 6:24; Romans 1:25

Guess what. Those things are your idols. You cared more about them than you did about obeying God. God said do not murder a person. People are sacrificing their children to the idol of abortion.

The land is polluted with blood. God has been bringing punishment gradually. When God finally pours His judgment on a rebellious nation, it's severe. There will be crying. Lots of crying – wailing – and gnashing of teeth. So much pain and misery – horror. Then some people will finally pray to God sincerely – and ask Him to kill them.
Revelation 6:15-17

As sure as I live, says the Lord, here's what I'll do.
You love to shed blood. So I'll make some blood for you.
But the blood I make will hunt you down.
God, Ezekiel 35:6

Chapter Nine

The Bible's simple facts

"Don't stop the children. Let them run to Me. The people in Heaven are like them."
Jesus, Matthew 19:14

Is a fetus a person?

• Isaac's wife Rebekah was pregnant with twin sons named Jacob and Esau. They were in her womb having a boxing match. The English word child or son in the Old Testament is most often translated from the Hebrew word ben.   Genesis 25:22

Jacob and Esau were born and grew up to be young men. Then one day, Rebekah took the clothing of her older son Esau and put it on Jacob her younger son. The word son in this verse is that Hebrew word ben. Two fully grown young men are called ben. And guess what they were called when they were in the womb. They were called ben. God didn't use a different word for them when they were in the womb.
                                                                        Genesis 27:15

God put Jacob and Esau in Rebekah's womb. And He knew what they would do with their lives. God knew those boys. Jacob and Esau were throwing punches at each other in the womb. Clearly, they were living human beings with feelings. They were people.   Genesis 25:21-23

• We see the same thing in the New Testament. In Luke 1:44, John the Baptist was leaping for joy. The reason John was so happy is that his Savior, Jesus Christ, had just come into the room.

Oh, there's something else I should tell you. John and Jesus were both in their mother's wombs at the time.

When John was jumping for joy in his mother Elisabeth's womb, the beloved physician Luke called John a child. The Greek word Luke used for child is brephos. Later on, in Luke 2:12, after Jesus had been born and was being held in His mother Mary's arms, Luke called Jesus a child, and Luke used the same Greek word, brephos. Colossians 4:14

God used the word brephos in these verses too –

•They brought infants (brephos) to Jesus so He would bless them.
                                    Luke 18:15

• In Acts 7:19, Stephen tells how the Egyptians killed the Israelite's young children (brephos). That happened in Exodus 1:22, when Pharaoh, Egypt's ruler, ordered that every son born to the Israelites was to be killed by throwing them in the river.

• Paul wrote this to Timothy –

> From the time you were a child (brephos)
> you have understood the holy Bible.
> There's power in the Bible
> – power to make you wise about salvation
> through faith – faith in Jesus Christ.
> 2 Timothy 3:15

• The apostle Peter wrote this –

> Like newborn babes (brephos), earnestly desire
> the pure milk found in the Bible
> so that by that milk you can grow into your salvation.
> 1 Peter 2:2

Once we're saved we need to grow into our salvation.

God says child. He makes no distinction. To God there's no difference. A child in the womb is a person – just as much a person as a child who's been born. God says brephos. God uses the one word, brephos, for a child in the womb and for children who've been born.

God's feelings of anger become so strong
that they burst forth from Heaven
against all those who have no respect for Him,
against those who know the truth – but don't share the truth.
God's vengeance falls upon them because
they love to do what He hates
– and they make it their mission to hide the truth from people.

Why is God so angry with them?
Because they have no excuse. Why not?
Because there are certain things about God,
certain truths that He wants everyone to know
– that He expects everyone to know.

God hasn't hidden these truths from anyone.
They're out in plain sight – they shine forth.
You can't miss them.
And God has put in every person
a built-in ability to see those truths.

God is in Heaven – people can't see Him.
But people can see God. How?
By looking around!
You can't see God in Heaven
but you can see God before your eyes
by observing this world He created.
Then you can understand that God is God
and that He has the ability to do anything
– He always has and He always will.

So, everybody knows God is there.
But a lot of people refuse to honor God as God
– people who don't want to think about God,
don't appreciate Him, and won't thank Him.
They let their minds go in useless directions
– and that makes them think they're smart.
But they're fools – there's no truth in their hearts.

Romans 1:18-22

Here's how I've rewarded you for rejecting My laws.
I placed certain people in your government.
What kind of people?
Let Me put it this way – those who were
born yesterday know Me better than they do.
I've given you leaders who have the
spiritual discernment of infants!
That's why you're having cruel laws forced on you.
God, Isaiah 3:4

The people are miserable when their king is a child.
Ecclesiastes 10:16

Life begins at conception –

> Your hands sculpted me. You shaped me like clay.
> You completed construction on my body.
> When You made my body it was like when someone pours milk
> into a container and then gradually turns the milk into cheese.
>
> You clothed me with skin and flesh.
> You gave me bones and tendons to protect me.
> You gave me life. And You gave me love.
> Your divine intervention guarded my breath.
> Job 10:8-12

That's Job's poetic description of what God did for him when he was in his mothers womb. Notice a few things. God gave Job life in the womb. God loved Job when Job was in the womb. And God intervened to guard Job's breath. The word breath is the Hebrew word ruach. It's the same word used for the Spirit of God. This passage shows how God feels about a child in the womb.

We have no right to destroy what God cares about so much.

Here's what king David said –

> It's You Lord who owns even my innermost being.
> It was You who knit me together in my mother's womb.
> Thank You. I'm in awe of You.
>
> I'm amazed at how miraculous Your work is.
> My very soul knows it's absolutely true.
> You could see my bones even when I was hidden
> and under construction.
>
> You saw me when You
> expertly weaved me together in my mother's womb.
> Your eyes saw me when I was just rolled up in a ball,
> before You unfolded me.

And even then – before I lived one day outside the womb,
You had already written in Your book
what you had planned for my life.

There's nothing more valuable to me than the plans
that You have for me, because You are God.
Psalm 139:13-17

Here's what God said to Jeremiah –

I already chose you before I formed you in the womb.
I set you apart before you came out of the womb,
and I ordained you to be a prophet to the nations.
God, Jeremiah 1:5

Can you see now why it's foolish to say abortion is okay because you can't determine for sure when life begins? Life begin at conception. But even if you claim you don't know, please look at that verse. God chose Jeremiah before Jeremiah was in his mother's womb. God separated Jeremiah to be a prophet before Jeremiah was born.

If you did an abortion on Jeremiah's mother you would have murdered someone that God knew, someone God chose and had plans for. God knew Jeremiah before Jeremiah was conceived in his mother's womb.

What happened from the time Jeremiah was conceived and the time he was born? Was he dead? No. He was a person before he was born, and during the nine months he spent in the womb. And he's still a person now, long after the death of his physical body. Jeremiah was Jeremiah, a person, the whole time he was in his mother's womb.
Matthew 22:32-33

Jeremiah never stopped being a person.

Your flesh body will become dust again.
And your soul that God put in your flesh body will go back to God.
Ecclesiastes 12:7

The Bloodyhands say a child in the womb can be aborted because they're not a person. They're saying we're as good as dead during the nine months we're in our mother's wombs. That's not true. The Bible says you're not even dead after you die. You came from God and you go back to God. You're never dead. The only way you can stop being alive is if God kills your soul in the lake of fire.

Matthew 10:28; Revelation 21:8

• There was a woman in Israel who had been unable to conceive. We're not told her name, but one day the Angel of the Lord appeared to her to tell her that now she will conceive and have a son.

The Angel told her that while she's pregnant she's not to drink any wine or strong drink. The reason the Angel gave is because a razor will never be put to her son's head. There was something special about that child. He was Samson, one of the saviors that God raised up in Israel to deliver them from their enemies.

Judges 13:3-5

There was a vow that a man or woman in Israel could choose to put themselves under. It was a vow to separate themselves to serve God. It's called the vow of a Nazirite. God put Samson under the vow of a Nazirite before Samson was conceived in his mother's womb.

While a person was under the vow of a Nazirite there were three things they couldn't do. They couldn't eat or drink anything that came from a grape vine, including grapes, raisins or any kind of beverage, including alcoholic beverages. They couldn't cut or shave off any of the hair on their head. And they couldn't go near a dead body.

Numbers 6:1-8

Notice that the Angel told her she was not to drink beverages made from grapes while she was pregnant. This wasn't for health reasons. It was because the child in her womb was under the vow of a Nazirite – even in the womb. This shows that the child in her womb was a person.

• God Himself decided to come to earth and live a life as a human being. He was named Jesus and His mother's name was Mary. An angel came to Joseph, Mary's husband, and told him that the Child in Mary's womb was conceived by the Holy Spirit.   Matthew 1:20

God's Holy Spirit didn't put a dead thing in Mary's womb. A dead thing doesn't turn into a living thing. Jesus was not dead when He was in Mary's womb. He was alive.

Think about it. God's Holy Spirit conceived Jesus in Mary's womb. Everything about that says life. God's Holy Spirit gives life.

You can't determine when life begins? What about Jesus? When He was in Mary's womb for nine months, was He alive or dead? Was He a person during the nine months He was in Mary's womb? Would you Bloodyhands be for or against aborting Jesus in Mary's womb?

Let me tell you. Jesus was a person when He was in the womb. Jesus was conceived differently than us but we were all people when we were in the womb just like Jesus was. Abortion murders a person.

• Before Ishmael, Isaac, John the Baptist, and Jesus were born, God had already chosen names for them. God told one of their parents what to name them. Were they nobody from conception to birth? No. They always were people.   Genesis 16:11; 17:19;
                              Matthew 1:21; Luke 1:13,31

God knows the child in the womb. He loves them. He carefully knits their body together. God never thinks of them as things. They are His children. Nothing can turn a child of God into a piece of garbage.

Chapter Ten

Don't let anyone deceive you

Look to our Guide

> Beware, don't let anyone deceive you.
> Jesus, Matthew 24:4

We have to remember how the Bloodyhands deceive. So I'll show you again how our Guide exposes their lying arguments. It's a matter of life and death. More children will be murdered tomorrow.

Keep your religion out of my uterus
So, are you in favor of murder, rape, and theft because religious people oppose them? Murder is illegal in atheistic countries. Will you say keep your atheism out of my uterus? And don't think you're innocent if you're an atheist. God said even those who never see a Bible will be held accountable.

You don't need religion to know it's wrong to reach into a woman's womb and kill the baby living there. It's not a religion thing. The truth can be seen by everyone through the conscience God gave us and by observing nature.   Romans 1:18-22; 2:11-16

Oppose abortion? Don't have one
So, I don't have to kill children? Oh, thanks. I should just mind my own business and let you go on killing children? No. I can't do that.

Back–alley abortions
They say – make abortion safe and legal. Because if you don't then women will suffer injuries and death in back-alley abortions.

Our Guide tells us what they're really saying – make murdering children safe and legal. Then women won't suffer injuries and death murdering children in a back-alley.

Emotional distress
They let a mother kill her child if she can convince a doctor that having the child might cause her emotional distress. Why don't they let the child be born so they can kill their mother? What about the emotional distress of being brought up by a mother who wanted you dead?

Obey the government
The Bible says Christians are supposed to obey the laws of their government. If abortion is legal then why don't Christians obey that law? Christians can't obey that law because it goes against a higher law, God's law – protecting children from being murdered.

The government can't legislate morality
Legislate means to make it a law. We have to legislate morality. Disagree? No, you don't. You want the government to legislate morality on men who think rape is right.

All laws involve morality. Morality is the rules of what's right and wrong. If the government didn't legislate morality then we would lose all our freedoms. That's why people need good government. The real question is whether abortion is right or wrong.

Everybody isn't free to do what they think is right. We live in a world of laws. The law takes away your freedom to sit in the park naked so it can protect other people's freedom to bring their kids to the park. That's legislating morality. The government is supposed to take away your freedom to get an abortion to protect the freedom of the child in your womb.

You Bloodyhands are legislating your morality on the child in the womb. You're telling the child – our morality says it's right to kill you and wrong to let you live. Bloodyhand morality results in the death of a child. That's why the government must stop abortion.

The government forces it morality on you when your morality murders people. The government can't let you have an abortion because of the right of the child in your womb to live so they too can enjoy the park. Children in the womb can't speak. It's up to us to speak for them.

Personal, intimate decision
A man is convicted of murder. He tells the judge it was a personal, intimate decision between him and his co-conspirators. The judge doesn't say – oh, in that case you're free to go. God, the Judge, doesn't excuse the murder of a child because it was personal and intimate.

The baby is unwanted

It's never right to murder someone to save someone else. I'm talking about murder. There are times, such as in war or in self-defense, when a life must be taken in order to save lives. That's not murder. But if your friend needs a kidney and you kill someone and take their kidney to save your friend's life – that's murder. And that's what most abortions are – the murder of a person to save someone else – to save them from the burden of having an unwanted baby.

Oppression of women

The Bloodyhands tell you about places in the world where women are forced to give birth. Hearing this stirs up anger in your chest and you become an abortion supporter. But you went by your heart and not your head. They manipulated you by playing on your feelings.

They tricked you by leaving out something – the millions of women who are being oppressed to death by those abortions you're now a supporter of. What they're really saying is that you're oppressing women if you don't let women murder women.

Women will argue that there was a time when contraceptives were less available. And many women were told by their church that they can't use contraceptives. So, women had no choice but to have baby after baby, year after year.

Now women say they want their rights – abortion on demand for any reason, without apology. That desire comes from the sinful old nature each of us has. To be able to make the right decision a woman needs her heart and mind changed by Jesus, the Bible, and God's Holy Spirit.

Adam and Eve invited sin, misery, and death into the world. One of the consequences of that is pain and suffering in childbirth. We caused that. Our sin made a mess of things. God said this to Eve after she disobeyed Him –

> I will greatly increase the suffering of having a child.
> Giving birth will be hard labor.
> God, Genesis 3:16

The Bible uses the word <u>travail</u> for giving birth. Travail is work that's painful and difficult. <u>But it's not all bad</u>. Jesus used the word travail when He met with His apostles on the night before He would be crucified.

Jesus told them that in a little while they would see Him no more. But then they would see Him again after a little while. The apostles didn't understand what Jesus meant, so they asked Him. And Jesus said this to the apostles –

> When a woman is in travail she feels pain
> because the baby is ready to arrive.
> But when they hand the child to her
> she forgets about the pain.
>
> She feels happiness because
> a child came into the world.
>
> And now you feel pain because I said I'm going away.
> But I will see you again,
> and then your heart will be filled with happiness.
> And no one will take that happiness from you.
>   Jesus, John 16:21-22
>
> Your pain will be turned into celebration.
>   Jesus, John 16:20

The child will have a bad life
There are actually people who say a child should be aborted to spare them from having a bad life. Would they want someone to make that decision for them? They'd scream – my rights! The child in the womb can't be heard. Shouldn't we let them be born and then ask them whether they'd rather be killed or risk having a bad life?

Women's health care
Abortion kills the little woman in the womb. What kind of women's health care is that? The morally correct choice, the healthy choice, is to let the child live. Do you know who suffers the most from abortion?

It's the women who have them. The children who are killed in the womb are in Paradise now enjoyng pleasures we can't imagine. So, kill them? No, we don't have the right to kill them.

Privacy

People in government said abortion must be made legal in order to protect a woman's right to privacy. Remember our Guide. The child in the womb is a person, no different than your five-year-old daughter. What if you killed her and you were brought to trial? Would the judge dismiss the case because of your right to privacy? The right to privacy doesn't turn evil into good.

If your concern is privacy then think about this. The child's privacy is violated when you invade their space to kill them. You'll have to answer to God for it. God has the right to intrude into your privacy any time He wants to. And God said the government must intrude into your privacy if you're planning a murder.

Women's rights

Can you see how they're deceiving you? The woman who has the abortion gets her rights and gets to go on with her life. The aborted child, that little woman, doesn't. She's dead now. The people who say they want abortion legal to protect women's rights – what are they doing? They're taking away the most important, most sacred right – the right to live, from the women they abort.

Can you see how they insult you? They think you're stupid. Prove them wrong. Look to the Truth. Which of the following would be a worse thing to happen to a woman? Giving birth to a baby? Or having intruders burst into her home at night, drag her out of her bed, violently attack her, and kill her? A pregnant woman has to deal with the first one. The tiny woman in the womb has to deal with the second one.

Is this getting to you? That's what abortion is. That aborted little girl doesn't get to grow up and live her life. She's dead. Yes, in some places girls are forced to marry men and get pregnant against their will.

Those kind of horrible things happen because of sinful people and bad governments. It's dishonest to use that as an argument for abortion. It still doesn't change the fact that abortion kills a child. It doesn't make it okay to use abortion as a form of birth control.

A war on women
The Bloodyhands say the Speakfors have declared a war on women. They say that for one reason – to stir up your feelings of righteous indignation. How dare they do that to women? After you calm down, stop and think. What did they do? They got you to not think about the fact that abortion is the gruesome murder of little women and men in their mother's womb. What about that war on women? How do you feel now that you know they toyed with your emotions to trick you?

> I am the truth. The truth will set you free.
> Jesus, John 8:32; 14:6

I didn't just feed you a fish. I taught you how to fish. Now you can expose lying arguments. You just need to learn how to look to our Guide. Look to the truth. Jesus is the Truth.

Why does God punish people?

I'll show you how God punishes disobedience and show you some reasons why. It's not just for Israel. The same principle applies to everyone. God made an example of Israel to teach us and warn us.

1 Corinthians 10:6

Here's what God said –

You must have a desire to escape from evil and care about
doing everything I've told you to do in the laws written in the Book.

But if you don't obey Me then you're not showing Me respect.
You're not standing in awe before the mighty and wonderful name
– THE LORD YOUR GOD.

And then, I, the Lord, will send strange afflictions to torment you
– strong and serious afflictions – and painful illnesses
for which there is no cure. They will hit you like lightning.

I will bring upon you all the diseases that made you afraid when I
brought them upon the Egyptians. Those diseases will stick to you.

And I will bring upon you every illness and every affliction which is
not written in the Book of the Law, until you are destroyed.

And if your descendants also refuse to obey Me
then they too will suffer the same punishment.
Deuteronomy 28:58-61

God punishes us to teach us and others a lesson. And God punishes us so we will cry out to Him. Thank God if He punished you. God punishes those He loves. He wants you to cry out to Him because He is eternal Life.

In 1 Corinthians 5:1-13, the apostle Paul told the Christians in Corinth to kick a man out of their church and send him to the devil. Why? Because the man was sleeping with his father's wife. It was obvious. Everybody in the church knew it but they let it continue. Why did Paul say send him to the devil?

So the man would become so oppressed by the devil that he would return to God. I said I'd show you reasons why God punishes people. That's one – so they will turn to God. God's chastening is true love.

See Hebrews 12:5-6 and Revelation 3:19

When the children of Israel went into the Promised Land there were still some of the previous occupants living there –

The Lord left those nations there so He could find out if the children of Israel would be faithful to Him and obey His laws.

Judges 3:4

People ask why God doesn't just kill the devil. Some ask why God doesn't kill all the evil people. Then He would have killed all of us. The day will come when God will kill the devil and all the evil people who won't obey Jesus. But for now, the devil and the evil people play an important part in God's plan. You can see a pattern in the Book of Judges –

1) The children of Israel did evil things.
   They did them out in the open,
   not caring that God could see what they were doing.
   They forgot about the Lord their God.
   And they obeyed the Canaanite gods instead.

Judges 3:7

God's anger was red hot toward them because of it.
So He put them in the hands of
the king of Mesopotamia,
who forced the children of Israel
to do hard work for eight years.

Judges 3:8

And the children of Israel cried out to the Lord.
So the Lord raised up a savior named Othniel
who rescued them.

Judges 3:9

2) The children of Israel did evil again,
not caring that God could see them.
Judges 3:12

And the Lord strengthened the king of Moab who
forced the children of Israel to serve him for eighteen years.
Judges 3:12-14

Then the children of Israel cried out to the Lord.
Judges 3:15

And the Lord raised up a savior named Ehud who rescued them.
Judges 3:15-30

---

3) After Ehud died the children of Israel once again did evil
in the sight of the Lord.
Judges 4:1

And the Lord sold the children of Israel into the hand of the king
of Canaan, who greatly oppressed them for twenty years.
Judges 4:2-3

And the children of Israel cried out to the Lord.
Judges 4:3

In Judges 4:4-24 we read how God used women this time,
Deborah and Jael, to rescue the children of Israel.

---

4) The children of Israel did evil in the sight of the Lord.

And the Lord put the children of Israel in the hands of
the Midianites, who oppressed them for seven years.
Judges 6:1-2

Then the children of Israel cried out to the Lord.
Judges 6:6

In Judges 6:7-7:25, God raised up a savior named Gideon
to rescue the children of Israel from the Midianites.

---

5) And the children of Israel did evil again in the sight of the Lord.
Judges 10:6

And the Lord's anger burned hot against them.
He sold them into the hands of the Philistines and the
Ammonites, who crushed the chidren of Israel
and oppressed them for eighteen years.
Judges 10:7-8

Then the children of Israel cried out to the Lord.
They said – we have sinned against You.
We have left our God and have obeyed
the Canaanite's gods instead.
Judges 10:10

And the Lord said to the children of Israel,
I delivered you from the Egyptians,
and from the Amorites, and the Philistines.

And when you were being oppressed by the Zidonians,
and the Amalekites, and the Maonites,
you cried out to Me, and I delivered you out of their hands.

But you have left Me again and obeyed the Canaanite gods.
So, I won't deliver you any more.
Go and cry to the gods that you've chosen.
Let them deliver you from your pain.

The children of Israel said to the Lord – we have sinned.
Do to us whatever You feel we deserve.
But please, rescue us today.
And the children of Israel turned away from the Canaanite gods
and obeyed the Lord.

The Lord could no longer bear to watch His people suffer.
So God used a man named Jephthah to rescue them.
Judges 10:11-16; 11:1-12:7

6) Then the children of Israel did evil again in the sight of the Lord.
Judges 13:1

And the Lord put them in the hands of the Philistines
who oppressed them for forty years.
Judges 13:1

In Judges 13:2–16:31, you can read how God caused a man
named Samson to rise up and rescue the children of Israel.

Why did this keep happening to the children of Israel? It's simple. God tells us twice in the Book of Judges. Everyone did was right in their own eyes. It means they didn't obey God's laws. Bad things happen whenever people break God's laws.

Everyone did what was right in their own eyes.
Judges 17:6

Everyone did what was right in their own eyes.
Judges 21:25

Why did God send people to oppress the children of Israel? Because He loved them. He knew that once their enemies got hold of them, that they would cry out to Him to rescue them. God is teaching us. He is showing us a pattern.

All of us left God so we could obey our idols. Our enemies are the devil and his ministers. God raised up the Savior, Jesus Christ. And when we cry out to Jesus, then He will deliver us from our enemies.

What we should learn from this is how serious it is to leave God and obey idols instead.

And we should realize how much God loves us. Look at what God did to deliver us. God Himself came and lived a perfect life in a human body.

He did that so He could die for us. That's love. God is love.

> God is love.
> 1 John 4:8,16

God is our Savior –

> If you will confess with your mouth that Jesus is Lord
> and believe in your heart that God raised Jesus from the dead,
> then you will be saved.
> Romans 10:9

Then you can say this –

> I thank You, God.
> You were angry with me
> but You've sent Your anger away
> and now You feel sorry for me.
>
> Everything has changed!
> With God as my salvation I'm safe and secure.
> I'm not afraid. God is my strength and my song.
> He rescued me.
>
> With joy I draw water out of the wells of salvation.
> Honor the Lord. Call to Him. Tell people what He can do.
> Make it known that God lives in the highest heights.
>
> Sing about the Lord.
> Make everyone in the world know about
> the excellent things He does.

Shout for joy. Sing joyfully you citizens of Jerusalem,
because great is the Holy One of Israel in your midst.
Isaiah 12:1-6

Jesus is the Holy One. And you're Israel if you believe in Jesus as your
Lord and Savior. You're a citizen of New Jerusalem. The apostle John
was shown what will happen when Jesus returns. John gave us this
description of what he saw –

I saw a new sky and a new earth.
The old sky and the old earth were gone
– they didn't exist any more.
And there were no more oceans, so all is calm.

And I John saw the holy city, New Jerusalem
coming down from God out of Heaven.
The city looked like a bride about to meet her husband.

And I heard a wonderful voice from Heaven saying,
Look! God will make His home with people.
He will live among them.
They will be His people,
and He will be their God with them.

And God's hands will wipe away all the tears from their eyes.
There won't be any more death
– there won't be any more mourning or crying
– and there won't be any more pain
because all those things are gone forever.
Revelation 21:1-4

If you received Jesus as your Lord and Savior then you're that bride –
the bride of Christ.

How to find some words and Bible verses –

In the <u>words</u> section the words are listed in alphabetical order.
In the <u>Bible verses</u> section the Bible verses are listed in the order
they appear in the Bible.

The first number after each word or Bible verse is the page
number where you'll find that word or verse.

Then there's a second number. It's in parenthesis ( ).
That's the number of the paragraph where you'll find
the word or verse. It will help you find what you're
looking for more quickly and easily

I'm not an expert in the science of numbering paragraphs.
I might count something that's one or two lines as a paragraph.
And I haven't necessarily been consistent in what I counted as a
paragraph. So just use the numbers as a direction finder.

If the number is (1), then it's at the top of the page.
The numbers (7) or (8) would be at the bottom.
Numbers (4) or (5) would be closer to the middle.
More or less.

Words ... Page numbers .. Paragraph numbers ( )

120

Bible verses....Page numbers...Paragraph numbers ( )

www.ingramcontent.com/pod-product-compliance
Lightning Source LLC
Chambersburg PA
CBHW021130020426
42331CB00005B/694